LAMDA

MUSICAL THEATRE

Exploring the World
Through Song

PUBLISHED BY
THE **LONDON ACADEMY**
OF **MUSIC AND DRAMATIC ART**

First published in 2007 by the
London Academy of Music and Dramatic Art
155 Talgarth Road, London W14 9DA
Tel: 0844 847 0520 / Fax: 0844 847 0521
e-mail: publications@lamda.org.uk
www.lamda.org.uk

A catalogue record for this book is available from the British Library.

ISBN: 978-0-9557687-0-5

Cover design: Society

Printed in Great Britain by Redlin, Chelmsford.

Contents

Foreword by Tim Rice   5

Introduction   7

Chapter One
Setting the Scene: A Brief Historical Introduction   9

Chapter Two
Light Opera and Operetta   13

Chapter Three
Music Hall and Vaudeville   30

Chapter Four
Jazz Musicals   44

Chapter Five
Book Musicals   54

Chapter Six
Concept Musicals   62

Chapter Seven
Pop and Rock Musicals   76

Chapter Eight
Preparation for LAMDA Examinations   89

Contributions for this publication were received from
Jayne Challinor, Jacque Emery, David Henson, Katrina
Mulvihill, Godfrey Salter and Carol Schroder.

Foreword

Musical theatre as we recognise it today comes from a very long tradition, made rich by the way it draws on a variety of different styles to make itself understood. An element of adaptability has allowed musical theatre to continue to be popular globally. Composers are continually developing their craft, exploring new ways of using music from across the world to allow the performer to help an audience understand the emotions he or she is portraying. Lyricists are also adapting the way words and phrases are delivered, using new and exciting speech patterns to more accurately demonstrate how a character is feeling.

At the root of a good musical is the writer's ability to match style to mood and the performer's ability to take the song and use it to tell a story to the audience.

Musical style has historically been used in this way. Opera often appeals to people who do not speak the language in which the opera is performed, because the music and performance accurately depict emotions so the audience understands what is happening. In the same way, the use of a particular style of musical theatre can set the audience in the correct frame of mind from the start.

It is the delivery of an overarching style that often helps an audience become absorbed in the performance. By taking the reader through six key musical theatre styles, this book opens the way to understanding how each of the styles developed historically and the impact they have continued to have. It covers light opera/operetta, vaudeville/ music hall, jazz, book, concept and pop/rock musicals, exploring their roots and recognising how elements are used in contemporary musical theatre. Exploring these styles will help any aspiring musical theatre performer to understand how musical theatre developed and in what way certain styles should be performed.

This book is an indispensable guide for those undertaking a LAMDA examination in Musical Theatre for the Actor/Singer and beyond this, it offers an interesting insight to key styles for teachers or students with an interest in musical theatre.

Tim Rice

Introduction

How does one actually define the art of musical theatre and why is it so popular? It is all things to many people, and this is, perhaps, the key to its popularity. It has songs, music, dialogue, dance, often lavish stage sets and/or costumes. It does provide that 'passport' to another world for a few hours – and offers its audience a chance to step inside a dream. It rarely deals with 'issues' in a way which a straight play often does and 'lifts' the audience, with memorable melodies and/or glamorous spectacle, into a world of sheer entertainment.

West End theatre is currently booming in the UK. In 2006 alone, audience figures were the highest ever, at 12.36 million. Based on figures produced from *The Daily Telegraph* newspaper, over the last 50 years a phenomenon has occurred regarding the expectations of the theatre-going public – the increased popularity of musical theatre. According to *The Daily Telegraph* in 1954 there were 6 musicals running in the West End, 2 revues and 28 straight plays and in 1974 there were 8 musicals, 1 revue and 27 straight plays. By 2004, however, the balance had shifted and there were 21 musicals and 18 plays. At the time of writing, in 2007, there are 26 musicals and only 13 plays*. If one also looks at planned future productions, according to The London Theatre Guide 36 musicals will be performed, as opposed to 39 straight plays. These figures mirror trends in the USA on Broadway.

The appetites of the viewing public have also been whetted by the presentation of reality TV competitions, such as the nationwide hunt to find a Maria for *The Sound of Music* (2006), Joseph for *Joseph and the Amazing Technicolor Dreamcoat* (2007) and Danny and Sandy for *Grease* (2007). The interest promoted by the television coverage and involvement through voting has brought musical theatre to a new audience in a way that Hollywood did in the 1930s and '50s. Even the controversial issues surrounding the Bollywood musical theatre star, Shilpa Shetty, with her appearance in 2007 on the Channel 4 programme, *Big Brother*, has promoted public interest in the genre for which she is famous.

The aim of this book is to explore all aspects of musical theatre – tracing its history and development from light opera into operetta, music hall and vaudeville, looking at its relationship with jazz, rock and pop music and the evolution of genres such as the book and concept musical. It is a fascinating journey – concluding with a chapter which provides students of all ages with an opportunity to work on their own performance skills.

If musical theatre is about transporting its audience into another world – it is about living the words and acting through song. Performers Meatloaf and Jason Donovan reiterated this in recent statements made on television, when giving advice to young performers. Jason Donovan said that *'the greatest singers in the world are not necessarily the most successful'* and that it was *'all about interpretation'***. On another occasion, Meatloaf encouraged singers to *'believe the words you are singing'* because *'you have to become that person'*. This identification with a character, or, in the words of Andrew Lloyd Webber, *'connection'*, is the key to believable performance – 'acting through song'. Mean what you sing… sing what you mean can be expanded to the dialogue and movement sequences too – the integrated whole should be 'in role'.

This is, perhaps, a far cry from the more fragmented origins of musical theatre, but it is the current 'footstep' on what has been a long and momentous journey. Whether you are candidates for the LAMDA Musical Theatre examinations or just interested in its evolvement, we invite you to join us in our exploration…

Notes

* *The Daily Telegraph*, Saturday 5th May 2007, 'Can We Keep the West End Glittering?'

** *Any Dream Will Do: The Search for Joseph* (BBC TV, March–June 2007).

Chapter One

Setting the Scene:
A Brief Historical Introduction

Throughout history we know that entertainment has always encompassed a good story with songs and dance, or any combination of all three. As far back as the 3rd Century BC Plautus included song and dance routines in his comedies. In the 5th Century BC there is evidence that songs were used by the Ancient Greeks, not only by the chorus to comment on the action centre-stage, but as part of the main plot and on occasion performed as a solo.

The Liturgical dramas of the 11th and 12th Centuries, such as *The Play of Herod* and *The Play of Daniel* included interludes of popular songs and slapstick humour to colour and lighten the religious texts.

By the Renaissance, these forms had evolved into commedia dell'arte, an Italian tradition where raucous clowns improvised their way through familiar stories, and from there, opera buffa developed. William Shakespeare clearly punctuated his plays with songs and music. In the late 1600s Molière turned several of his comedies into musical entertainments with songs, the music being composed by Jean Baptiste Lully.

Strolling players had been touring the British Isles for many years, telling stories through song and dance. They started to form companies and build their own theatres. London became the principal centre and the hub of theatrical development. Players were sent on tour to other major centres such as Manchester, Birmingham, Edinburgh and Dublin; again, theatres were built to accommodate these companies.

New York's first-known professional musical production was John Gay's ballad opera, *The Beggar's Opera*, offered by Walter Murray and Thomas Kean's travelling theatrical troupe at the Nassau Street Theatre on December 3rd, 1750. This tells a story; it has a beginning, a middle and an end so could come under the title of a book musical, but it falls more snugly under its own genre of an opera because of the style of music and the technical expertise expected of its vocalists.

Around this time strolling troupes, often made up of family members, arrived in America from London. Lewis Hallam's Company of Comedians arrived in 1752 and renamed themselves The American Company. It was families such as the Hallams, travelling from town to town, that eventually settled down and built the theatres we know today in the larger towns and cities all over America.

In England the popularity of melodrama was fed by the fact that many theatres were licensed only as music halls and not allowed to present plays without music, whilst in America the revolution of 1774 tried to curtail theatrical activities, yet concerts with a musical element were allowed to continue. So, under the guise of 'musical entertainment', drama continued and developed.

The theatre relied heavily on the musical element of entertainment. An evening would consist of a short musical concert of 'waiting' music played by an orchestra. This would be followed by a prologue and then the main work, concluding with a shorter light entertainment piece in the form of a farce or pantomime. Between each section the orchestra would play short interludes; these eventually developing into musically accompanied song or dance. When the main piece was a ballad or comic opera, the musical element grew, as did the staging.

The American scene of the 18th Century reflected the happenings of the theatre world in the British Isles. The American theatres became important competitors with the provincial theatres of England. Actors, actresses and even pantomime artists, most of whom were French, would arrive in England and be tempted onto the American scene. The

American producers and directors would copy the English theatrical repertoire even going as far as copying the costumes and scenery. One of the most important tasks of the American musical director was to re-orchestrate the musical accompaniments, compose new incidental music, or even completely rewrite the music of the English repertoire.

The early 1800s saw the birth of Broadway. New York's growing population developed a passion for the theatre and producers were happy to cater to this growing audience. Theatres were built along the main street – Broadway – and melodramas became increasingly popular. During this period, music, co-ordinated with lavish scenic designs and lighting effects, was not only used as an accompaniment to song, but also used to heighten the emotional element.

The most popular musical stage shows of the early and mid 19th Century were the minstrel shows. Thomas Rice introduced the song (and character) 'Jump Jim Crow' in the early 1830s. In 1842, a group of four unemployed actors who had experience doing 'blackface routines' in circuses banded together to present a full evenings entertainment. Calling themselves The Virginia Minstrels, their 'plantation songs', stories and shuffling dances were a sensation. Minstrel troupes soon toured the country telling the story of the American Black African and slavery in song. Over the next few years, The Virginia Minstrels introduced several hit songs that are still heard today, including 'Polly Wolly Doodle' and 'Blue Tail Fly'.

The mid 19th Century saw many varied musical productions that encompassed a plot (which at times was rather loose or tenuous), song and dance, but no one actually called them 'musicals'. A play with songs might advertise itself as a burletta, extravaganza, spectacle, operetta, comic or light opera, pantomime or even parlour opera.

It is commonly accepted, however, that it was *The Black Crook* (1866) that first conformed to the modern concept of a 'musical'. With original music by Thomas Baker, the production lasted for over five hours! Despite its length, it ran for a record-breaking 474 performances and included melodrama, fantasy, ballet and elaborate sets and staging. This marriage of styles was the result of an accident when a theatre burned down, leaving 100 French dancers without a venue or a production. It was the manager of Biblo's Garden Theatre who decided to merge his melodrama with the dance. Its success resulted in the creation of other similar extravaganzas, but only Edward Everett Rice's *Evangeline* or *The Belle of Arcadie* (1874), with elements of burlesque, minstrelsy and comic opera, rivalled the popularity of *The Black Crook*. The latter was even used by Sigmund Romberg in 1954 for the inspiration of *The Girl in Pink Tights*.

This brief historical background sets the scene for the chapters to come, which explore individual styles and categories in detail and looks at their specific contexts, influences and impact on the exciting evolvement of musical theatre.

Chapter Two

Light Opera and Operetta

INTRODUCTION

Light opera and operetta – for many people the very words conjure up images of lightweight songs, caricature characters and absurd situations with trivial plots set in fantasy lands in Middle Europe. For others, however, they have become a way of life and a *raison d'être* for many amateur operatic societies. They conjure up sounds of rousing choruses, witty lyrics and opportunities to display vocal skills – from dexterity in executing an intricate aria to the crisp articulation required in the presentation of artless patter. Whatever one's musical taste, however, it cannot be denied that the art form is both as popular today as it ever was – with current revivals of key operettas – and it has played a pivotal role in the evolvement of modern musical theatre.

DEFINITIONS AND ORIGINS

'Light opera' or 'comic opera' denotes a sung drama of a light or comic nature. It first developed in late 18th Century Italy as opera buffa as opposed to opera seria or serious, traditional opera. At first, comic operas were presented as interludes between acts of more serious works. They then developed into a completely independent art form. In England, its equivalent was the ballad opera. This consisted of humorous, often satirical spoken dialogue, interspersed with short songs. Unlike other forms of light opera, the tunes were usually well-known and contemporary – a mixture of broadsheet ballads (which gave them their name), operatic arias, hymns and folk songs.

The word 'operetta' literally means 'little opera' and it denotes sung material that concentrates on the lighter elements of opera, such as subject and style and, more importantly, includes some spoken dialogue. In mid 19th Century Paris, the French government set up a law which limited the number of performers to three and the length of performance to one act in a bid to deter independent productions. However, this only encouraged the composer Jacques Offenbach to lease his own theatre. The Théâtre des Bouffes-Parisiens saw the presentation of a series of one-act comic musicals which he called operettas. In 1858, with the three singer ban lifted, he wrote the first full scale operetta, *Orphée aux Enfers* (*Orpheus in the Underworld*).

HISTORICAL OUTLINE AND EXAMPLES

There were several cultural differences which affected the development of light opera and operetta, and a variety of styles evolved – English light or comic opera; French, German, Viennese and American operettas.

In England, ballad opera was one of the most obvious predecessors of the modern musical. A work conforming to the original genre would include music from contemporary pop songs linked together. This had an impact on the development of light opera as it appealed to a wider audience than the more serious opera which was sung in Italian. The most famous of the ballad operas – and the one to have stood the test of time – was John Gay's *The Beggar's Opera* (1728), with music arranged by Johann Christoph Pepusch. The original idea of the opera came from Jonathan Swift who wrote a letter to Gay, suggesting; 'What think you of a Newgate pastoral among the thieves and whores there?' Gay thought that a comedy would be better than a pastoral. The storyline looks at the upper classes and their passion for Italian opera, social inequality and the contrast between the lives of the aristocracy and those of 'thieves' and 'whores'. In 1928 Bertolt Brecht and Kurt Weill created a new musical adaptation of the work and called it *The Threepenny Opera*. The only song to appear in both operas is that of Peachum, the self-justified thief catcher, sitting at his account books. *The Beggar's Opera* has been revived many times and it ran for 1,463 performances at London's Lyric Theatre in 1920.

During the latter half of the 19th Century, the world of operetta was dominated by the work of Jacques Offenbach in France, Johann Strauss II in Vienna and W.S. Gilbert and Arthur Sullivan in England.

Offenbach joined the librettists Henri Meilhac and Ludovic Halevy to produce *Orfee* (1858). Most of Offenbach's operettas combined firm melodic lines with political satire. Although Orfee does retell the Greek legend of Orpheus descending into Hades to save his beloved Eurydice, it pokes fun at Gluck's serious opera about the same characters. After his initial success with Orfee, Offenbach went on to compose 100 operettas. His output was so prolific that he sometimes used the same material in more than one operetta. The 'Can Can', or 'Infernal Gallop', became an immediate sensation and is still associated with popular music in Paris today. Other successful operettas he composed were *La Belle Hélène* (1864), which provided a comic account of the story of Helen of Troy, and *La Grande Duchesse de Gerolstein* (1867). The latter is a political satire about a flirtatious noblewoman who was very fond of any man in a uniform. It was first performed in New York and caused Offenbach to become an immediate celebrity. When the reign of Napoleon II ended in 1870, he decided to leave France and tour Britain and the United States. Composers like Charles Lecocq carried on the tradition of French operetta. In spite of the fact that Lecocq's operetta, *La Fille de Madame Angot* (1872), became one of the most popular of its time, it is seldom performed today. Offenbach's work, however, crossed national boundaries and became very popular, especially in Vienna, having a profound influence on future generations of composers.

Johann Strauss II, a well-known composer of dance music and the son of Johann Strauss I, who had popularised the Viennese waltz, wanted to write an operetta of his own. Inspired by the work of Offenbach and encouraged by his wife, singer Henrietta Treffz, his first operetta was *Indigo und die Vierzig Rauber* (1871). He went on to write 15 more. They all have a very distinctive Viennese musical style with waltzes, polkas and marches within them. His most influential operetta, however, was his third: *Die Fledermaus (The Bat)* (1874). It had a German libretto by Carl Haffner and Richard Genee and was based on a farce by Julius Benedix and a French play, *Le Réveillon*, by Offenbach's librettists, Henri Meilhac and Ludovic Halevy. *Die Fledermaus* is a story about a man who, after a night of heavy drinking, is left by a Viennese roadside wearing a bat costume. The operetta tells of the practical jokes played by this man as a means of revenge on his so-called 'friend' who left him on the roadside in the first place. Initially the operetta was more popular in Berlin than it was in Vienna but it grew in popularity and became one of the most performed operettas in the world. It is, in fact, claimed by Opera America as the nineteenth most performed opera in America. Arguably its most famous aria is the song of the maid, Adele, 'The Laughing Song', in which she pokes fun at Eisenstein. There are about 20 recordings of *Die Fledermaus*, including Herbert von Karajan (1955) and Andre Prévin (1990). It has also been adapted several times for the cinema and for television, for example in the British film *Oh Rosalinda* (1955).

Viennese operetta reached its climax in 1905 with *Die Lustige Witwe (The Merry Widow)*. Composed by Hungarian-born Franz Lehar, it is a romantic musical comedy set in an imaginary Central European country and is about a rich widow and her attempts to find a husband. The librettists, Victor Leon and Leo Stein, based the story on the comedy *L'Attaché d'Ambassade* by Henri Meilhac. The English adaptation was by Basil Hood, with lyrics by Adam Ross. It is reputed that King Edward VII attended four performances when it opened in London at the Daly Theatre in 1907. It crossed the Atlantic in October of that year during a period of great financial insecurity. In spite of this, the opera was given excellent publicity. Sheet music was readily available, touring companies played its waltzes and Merry Widow hats, with broad brims and feather trims, created a fashion craze! When De Koven from the New York World newspaper attended the American premiere he did not know what a lasting success the operetta would enjoy. He did write, however, that:

> 'The dramatic purpose and coherency, the artistic sincerity... shown in The Merry Widow last night, came like water in the desert after the tawdry musical insanities which have pervaded...Broadway for some years...It is (the) artistic unity in purpose and dramatic treatment that is the controlling factor in the success which the opera has obtained the world over.'

The Merry Widow has been played frequently throughout the English-speaking world. Well-known music from the score includes 'The Merry Widow Waltz' and 'Vilja'.

However, it was English light opera that was to play a pivotal role in the development of future writing for musical theatre, as it was to be revolutionised at the end of the 19th Century. Since The Beggar's Opera, the London stage had been dominated by a mixture of burlesque and pantomimes. Offenbach's French operettas became popular, but in the 1870s a legendary musical partnership was born. John Hollingshead was responsible for the first collaboration between W.S. Gilbert and Arthur Sullivan when he needed musical entertainment for the Gaiety Theatre in 1871. The 'Operatic Extravaganza' which followed was not particularly successful, but four years later, Richard D'Oyly Carte commissioned them to write a one-act opera to follow an evening of Offenbach's short operetta La Périchole (1875). The result was Trial by Jury, which was a complete success. D'Oyly Carte's Opera Bouffe Company took it on tour and Gilbert and Sullivan were commissioned to write a full-length opera, The Sorcerer (1877). They went on to compose 14 operettas, or light operas as they were known in England at the time, and created a musical style whose influence is still as strong in the 21st Century as it was when it began.

Gilbert and Sullivan also had a huge impact in the United States. The 1878 Boston premiere of *HMS Pinafore* was a turning point in the history of American musical theatre, and within a year more than 90 companies toured with it in the United States alone. This infatuation was known as 'Pinafore-Mania'. Gerald Bordman claims that *Pinafore* itself

'determined the course and shape of the popular lyric stage in England and America for the final quarter of the nineteenth century.'

HMS Pinafore, or *The Lass That Loved a Sailor*, is the story of a naval captain's daughter who rejects the love of the First Lord of the Admiralty because she loves an ordinary sailor. It mocked the Victorian class system and, in a jocular way, the Royal Navy. Some disapproval of its content made its success a little slow in London, but cleverly, Sullivan's summer concerts played some of the key tunes from the score and the operetta's popularity grew. It became so popular that D'Oyly Carte's investors tried to steal the production from him and sent gangs to carry off the sets and costumes in the middle of a performance! There was a scuffle and both cast and crew fought them off. It was as a direct result of this, however, that D'Oyly Carte formed an exclusive partnership with Gilbert and Sullivan. Many of Pinafore's songs were whistled and sung on both sides of the Atlantic, in particular, 'Little Buttercup', and Sir Joseph's patter song, 'When I Was a Lad'. The operetta also became a source of popular expressions, such as the exchange:

'What, never?'

'No never!'

'What, never?'

'Well, hardly ever!'

The Pirates of Penzance or *The Slave of Duty* (1879) was written as an expression of annoyance at the American copyright pirates. It also poked fun at 'a sense of duty' and conventions associated with Grand Opera. D'Oyly Carte secured the first international copyright by premiering it simultaneously in New York and London. Even though illegal productions still took place, they were fought in the courts and actually established legal precedents that protect writers and composers over 100 years later. *The Pirates of Penzance* is a story about a young man who is accidentally apprenticed to a band of pirates by a confused nursemaid. From the beginning, *The Pirates of Penzance* has been one of Gilbert and Sullivan's most popular comic operas. Prophetically, in a letter to his mother about the new opera upon which he was at work in New York, on December 10th, 1879, Sullivan wrote:

'I think it will be a great success, for it is exquisitely funny and the music is strikingly tuneful and catching.'

Key musical numbers include 'When Fred'ric was a Little Lad', 'Poor Wand'ring One', and the patter song, 'I am the Very Model of a Modern Major General'.

The Mikado (1885) was influenced by a craze for Japanese memorabilia. Although set in Japan, it was really a send-up of British customs and pretensions. The plot centres around the decree that the Emperor of Japan has made flirting a crime punishable by death. Songs like 'The Sun Whose Rays', 'Three Little Maids', 'A Wand'ring Minstrel' and 'Titwillow' have become well-known and are just as popular today as they were in 1885. It is interesting to note that *The Mikado* is the only one of the Gilbert and Sullivan operettas to be widely performed in languages other than English, and it remains one of the most frequently produced. It is also one of the few to have caused any diplomatic problems. During his visit to Britain in 1907, the crown prince of Japan requested that he would like to see a performance of *The Mikado*. Unfortunately, it was thought to be insensitive and had been banned for the duration of his visit.

English operetta continued with such works as Stephenson and Cellier's *Dorothy* (1886) and German and Hood's *Merrie England* (1902). The former was purchased by the producer George Edwardes and it actually ran for longer than any Gilbert and Sullivan opera. Its genre was somewhere between comic opera and musical comedy. Edwardes ran a series of musical comedies that would pack the Gaiety Theatre for many years to come. When *The Gaiety Girl* (1893) reached Broadway in 1894 the British chorus of Gaiety Girls brought the house down! The scores of these shows all bore a certain resemblance and were variations on one basic theme. As Noel Coward later wrote:

> *'In most of these entertainments there was nearly always a bitter misunderstanding between the hero and the heroine at the end of the first act...The ultimate reconciliation was usually achieved a few seconds before the final curtain. I still long to hear the leading lady cry with a breaking heart, "...play louder... I want to dance and forget!"'*

Musically, these shows would have the same 'sound' as earlier light operas, and require the same vocal technique, but the later ones developed a different 'style' of presentation.

In America, Victor Herbert and John Philip Sousa wrote operettas whose styles were influenced by that of Gilbert and Sullivan. Sousa, known as 'the march king', wrote 15 operettas. His most famous, *El Capitan* (1896), is remembered for its famous march.

Another composer, Reginald De Koven, joined the librettist Harry B. Smith and had some success with comic operas such as *Wang* (1891), starring the comedienne Della Fox as a male character, and *Robin Hood* (1891), which featured the song 'Promise Me' – a ballad that became a favourite choice at wedding ceremonies across America. Harry B. Smith had a career spanning over 40 years as a lyricist, in which he wrote the librettos for 123 Broadway musicals.

Victor Herbert, Irish by birth, German by education and American by choice, was arguably the most successful American composer of comic opera at the turn of the 20th Century. His operetta, *The Red Mill* (1906), with a libretto by Henry Blossom, was a great success. The score contains some of Herbert's most famous tunes, including 'The Streets of New York'. The plot involves two American comedians abroad and forbidden love, undisclosed fortunes, and, as in many operettas, opportunities for disguise! One of Herbert's later works, *Naughty Marietta* (1910), starred the Italian opera singer Emma Trentini. Songs such as, 'I'm Falling in Love with Someone', and the duet, 'Ah! Sweet Mystery of Life' were made famous much later when Naughty Marietta was filmed by the Hollywood singing duo Nelson Eddy and Jeannette MacDonald in 1935.

The next few years were dominated by the upheavals and hardships of World War I. Operetta and light opera could be perceived by some to be 'necessary escapism', but also by many as sheer frivolity. It prompted several important European composers to emigrate to the United States – notably Sigmund Romberg and Rudolf Friml – both of whom were to play key roles in the evolvement of operetta and eventually, the 'Musical'. However, anti-German sentiments were strong in both the United Kingdom and America. There was a reaction against plots set in a Germanic Central European country, albeit an imaginary one. Interestingly, whilst Romberg's *The Student Prince* (1924) did not do as well in London because of this, it was still a great success in New York and ran for 608 performances on Broadway.

The 1920s saw the dominance of American operetta, with its romance and musical heritage providing the backdrop to the 1940s – the rise of the 'Golden Age of the Broadway Musical'. Common to most operettas was the inclusion of specific types of music – waltzes, marches, choruses and love duets. Their storylines were unrealistic, exotic and very romantic. Romberg adapted the melodies of Franz Schubert for *Blossom Time* (1921) which was produced in England as *Lilac Time*. Whilst this was very successful, his key operettas – which have stood the test of time – are *The Student Prince* (1924) and *The Desert Song* (1926). His musical style was similar to that of Lehar. The book and lyrics of *The Desert Song* were written by Oscar Hammerstein II and Otto Harbach respectively. The story is set in Morocco and concerns the handsome Red Shadow, leader of a band of rebels who threaten the safety of a French outpost. There are several key songs within the operetta but possibly 'The Desert Song' and 'The Sabre Song' are the most well known. The operetta has been adapted for television and made into a film four times – the most famous being in 1955 with Kathryn Grayson and Gordon MacRae. To celebrate the centenary of Romberg's birth, in 1987 the New York City Opera staged a special production starring Richard White and Linda Michele.

Another key operetta from 1924 was *Rose Marie*. With music by Rudolf Friml and Herbert Stothart and lyrics by Oscar Hammerstein II and Otto Harbach, it was one of the first operettas to be set in North America – with the Canadian Rockies as its backdrop. The story concerns a singer, Rose Marie, and her love for a man, who has gone into hiding after being accused of murder. According to William Everett, Friml took advice from his mentor, the composer Dvorak, and incorporated certain Indian musical sounds into the score – such as a strong driving beat, the use of drone fifths and chromaticism. The opening of the famous 'Indian Love Call' is an example of the effect of the latter. Both Romberg and Friml displayed different musical influences in the development of their own individual styles. Romberg was clearly linked to Viennese operetta and Friml more to British roots. American operetta was affected by external events in the late 1920s. The stock market crash of 1929 and the ensuing period of the Great Depression affected audience desire and expectation. Colourful large-scale productions became too expensive and the viewing public wanted nothing but humour.

British audiences also wanted to get away from post-war gloom and 'non-Ruritanian' musical theatre provided an escape mechanism. The operetta *Chu Chin Chow* (1916), with music by Frederick Norton and book and lyrics by Oscar Asche, actually premiered whilst World War I was still being fought. It was an Arabian Nights fantasy and eventually played for five years (2,235 performances) in London. Its star was the actress and singer Jose Collins, who also went on to be the leading lady in the other important British operetta of the time, *The Maid of the Mountains* (1917) – with music by James Tate, book by Frederick Lonsdale and lyrics by Harry Graham. It was a great success in London because its setting was one of fantasy and a chance to escape from reality. It tells the story of lovers and outlaws in a fictitious land of brigands. The key song, 'Love Will Find a Way', is often sung today but unfortunately the operetta did not enjoy the same amount of success and only played for 37 performances in New York. Whilst the 1920s were dominated by Americans in general, two key British composers emerged in the next decade and carved an important niche in the evolvement of British musical theatre. They were both colourful and flamboyant characters and, arguably, the last of the British composers of 'true' operetta. The first of these was Noel Coward, whose first success was *Bitter Sweet* (1929). His musical style in the operetta is varied and includes the Charleston and a Viennese waltz like 'Zigeuner'. Another key song is 'I'll See You Again'. It is set in Vienna and is told as a flashback. It is both a bitter and sweet story about a singer, Sari, who eloped with a young music teacher who is murdered not long after their marriage. Many of Coward's individual songs feature in concerts and have found lasting success – especially some of his patter songs, for example, 'Mad Dogs and Englishmen', but it could be argued that his musical style often varied from the genre of operetta found in *Bitter Sweet*.

In contrast, the second of the two key British composers, Ivor Novello developed a distinctive musical style which is found in all his operettas. He first became famous with his music for the song, 'Keep the Home Fires Burning', which became an anthem of World War I. He found success as an actor on both stage and screen and regularly appeared in his own musical compositions. Novello is known today for many of his songs such as 'Waltz of My Heart', 'Someday My Heart Will Awake' and 'We'll Gather Lilacs'. His eight principal operettas included *Glamorous Night* (1935),

Careless Rapture (1936), *The Dancing Years* (1939) and *King's Rhapsody* (1949). According to John Snelson, the image of a Novello show was:

> '*overtly emotive in music, romantically idealised in plot and rich in visual impact.*'

One of his most successful and best remembered operettas was *The Dancing Years*. The number, 'Lorelei', shows the influence of Lehar and 'I Can Give You the Starlight', Romberg. It is 'Waltz of My Heart', however, that has probably been Novello's most performed solo song. The plot of *The Dancing Years* concerns a composer, originally played by Novello, who falls in love with an opera singer. It is an affair which is beset with problems and misunderstandings in true operetta style. Novello made his main character an Austrian Jew in order to make a statement about the Nazi regime. The management tried to get him to change this, as they believed that it was inappropriate for a musical, but Novello refused. Ironically, its initial production in London only ran for 187 shows – not because of its lack of popularity – but because of the outbreak of World War II. Initially all West End theatres closed down, but soon reopened with morale-raising entertainment including well-loved repeats of operettas such as *The Desert Song*, *Chu Chin Chow*, *Rose Marie* and *The Merry Widow*. *The Dancing Years* opened again in 1942 and ran for two years with 969 performances.

OPERETTA – FROM STAGE TO SCREEN

The late 1920s saw the beginning of the importance of Hollywood as a centre for motion pictures. This was also, arguably, the time when operetta as a genre was at its most popular. Operetta-loving audiences were given the opportunity to escape into their musical dreams within the confines of the cinema, to some extent echoed by the popularity of the Bollywood musical today.

Hollywood, therefore, played an important role in the development of operetta and its accessibility. Altogether, there were 14 film operettas produced during this period. The first was *The Desert Song* (1929), produced by Warner Brothers, starring John Boles, Carlotta King and Myrna Loy. The film remained faithful to the original script but other versions changed the plot – such as the 1943 adaptation which included Nazis in the North African desert!

In *The New Moon* (1930), the story was completely rewritten, as it was in the 1936 version of *Rose Marie*. The latter starred Jeannette MacDonald and Nelson Eddy and, as with the majority of their film operettas, the storyline was changed to allow them to sing all key songs. This famous singing duo made eight film operettas together. They were nicknamed 'The Beauty and the Baritone' or 'America's Singing Sweethearts' and were often identified with the romantic lovers they portrayed. They achieved tremendous celebrity status and served as role models for aspiring actor/singers of the day. Their films included *Naughty Marietta* (1935), *Rose Marie* (1936) and *Bitter Sweet* (1940). Film versions of operettas continued to be screened until the 1950s – with classic remakes of *The Desert Song* (1953) and *The Vagabond King* (1956) – but by then, the viewing public were beginning to become interested in a different form of musical theatre on film.

CONNECTIONS

It is often hard to say exactly where an operetta ends and a 'book' musical or musical comedy begins. In 1927, Jerome Kern and Oscar Hammerstein II wrote *Show Boat*, which is often considered to be the beginning of the musical play. It still required singers who could sustain a difficult melodic line, but above all, it had a less far-fetched narrative. Based on Edna Ferber's novel of the same name, the story raised a number of issues about relationships between races (in a pre Civil Rights America). Although the cast was mixed-race there was no attempt at any form of stereotyping, as there had been in *Rose Marie* only a few years earlier. As a musical play it was successful and its tunes memorable, although musically it is a pastiche, because Kern composed music in a variety of styles to reflect the different times in which the story was set. He even utilised well-known tunes by composers such as John Philip Sousa and Charles K. Harris. However, songs like 'Ole Man River' and 'Can't Help Lovin' Dat Man of Mine' had travelled a long way from the influence of 'Ruritania'.

Even further removed from the world of operetta, yet distinctly rooted in opera, and an operatic vocal style, were two great musicals of the era – George and Ira Gershwin's folk opera, *Porgy and Bess* (1935), based on the novel *Porgy*, by Dorothy and Edwin DuBose Heyward, and Oscar Hammerstein II's rearrangement of Bizet's opera *Carmen* into *Carmen Jones* (1942). Both operas are also concerned with African American storylines. *Porgy and Bess* depicts the harsh and violent life of Catfish Row on the Charleston waterfront, with its gambling, murders, fugitives and hurricanes. Songs like 'Summertime' and the emotional love duet between Porgy and Bess have become classics in their own right and Gershwin stuck to an operatic formula using sung recitative instead of dialogue to move the action of the plot and link key songs. In *Carmen Jones*, Hammerstein turned the original opera into an opera with dialogue and replaced the recitative. The action was also transferred from a cigarette factory in Seville to a parachute factory in the southern United States. Hammerstein's new lyrics were set to Bizet's original music. This was a critical point in the lyricist's career and in a new-found partnership with composer, Richard Rodgers, a new era began in the history of the musical. The result of their initial collaboration was *Oklahoma!* (1943). The music followed the plot and development of the storyline and there were no modifications to keep in line with particular musical styles. The world of the operetta had finally been eclipsed.

THE WAY FORWARD

Popular operettas such as *The Pirates of Penzance*, *Die Fledermaus* and *The Merry Widow* have stood the test of time in their entirety. Others are best remembered for key songs within them and some have long been forgotten. As a genre and art form, however, the influence of light opera and operetta on the development of musical theatre today cannot be denied. Its popularity peaked both in the time of Gilbert and Sullivan and again in the 1920s. Lyricists like Oscar Hammerstein II straddled both operettas and Broadway musicals, with his involvement in *Rose Marie* and *The Desert Song* as well as *Oklahoma!* and *South Pacific*. Specific songs such as 'One More Kiss' from Stephen Sondheim's *Follies* (1971) and 'Music of the Night' from Andrew Lloyd Webber's *Phantom of the Opera* (1986) have their roots in a classical heritage. Memorable melodies, technically well delivered, may indeed linger in the memory and inspire new generations of composers to musical theatre. Perhaps one of the charms of operetta lies in the fact that themes such as honour, duty, love and beauty – however fleeting – are passports to escapism and have their own timeless value. An editorial tribute to Jeannette MacDonald in the San Diego Evening Tribune summarised this by saying;

> *'Songs like 'Rose Marie' and 'Indian Love Call' espoused no great causes…That was part of their appeal…and that anyone could, for a moment at least, taste something of the 'Sweet Mystery of Life'.*

This is their true legacy.

VOCAL STYLES

The cult of celebrity existed long before the present day. The 18th Century saw the rise of the theatrical star and the 19th Century, the vocal star. These early singers performed both in concerts and as guests with visiting opera companies. They toured extensively and the public flocked to hear them and buy sheet music of the songs they performed. These singers took leading roles in English comic operas as well as in more traditional operas such as those by Rossini and Mozart. The technical agility of some of the coloratura sopranos had a major impact on audiences. This was the calibre of the singers who performed in the first light operas and operettas – singers like Lucille Tostee, Caroline Ritchings and Hortense Schneider.

In order to cope with the range and phrasing in the majority of operetta solos, a classically-trained vocal technique is usually required. Consequently, most key performers have been singers who could act as opposed to actors who could sing. The demands of the songs outweighed those of the dialogue and some, like the great Jessie Bond, had to be coaxed into speaking on stage. Several of the characters in the storylines were indeed singers such as Sari in *Bitter Sweet* and Maria in *The Dancing Years* and some songs had actually been composed with certain trained opera singers in mind, such as Emma Trentini in *Naughty Marietta*. It could be argued that the difference in vocal style between operetta/ light opera and a musical is that the former is 'light opera with acting' and the musical, 'a play with singing'. Whilst this is best seen in the casting of performers, many great musical artistes have been well-known opera singers. For example, in the past, Enzio Pinza, known for his performance as *Don Giovanni*, appeared in *South Pacific* on Broadway and Constance Shacklock, the British Wagnerian mezzo-soprano, was Mother Abbess in London's first production of *The Sound of Music* (1961). This tradition continued with cross-over artistes such as Lesley Garrett, Mother Abbess in the 2007 production.

DISCUSSION POINTS

• *What is an operetta?*

• *Can you give an example of a light opera or operetta which has had a direct influence on the musical theatre of today?*

• *How did operetta begin as an art form and when was it at its most popular?*

• *What external political influences restricted the choice and development of operetta in France, England and the United States?*

• *Why do you think Gilbert and Sullivan are still so popular today?*

• *What style of singing is required to perform light opera and operetta? How does this differ from other forms of musical theatre?*

REFERENCES

Brockes, Emma – *What Would Barbra Do?: How Musicals Changed My Life* HarperCollins Publishers, 2007

Everett, William A. & Laird, Paul R. (eds.) – *The Cambridge Companion to the Musical* Cambridge University Press, 2002

Phaidon – *Phaidon Book of the Opera* Phaidon Press Ltd., 1978

Tebbutt, Gerry – *Musical Theatre* Dramatic Lines, 2003

Walmisley, Claude A, & Walmisley, Guy H. – *'Tit-willow' or Notes and Jottings on Gilbert and Sullivan Operas* C.A. Walmisley, 1964

http://en.wikipedia.org

http://musicaltheatreguide.com

www.musicals101.com

www.musical-theatre.net/index.html

www.stagebeauty.net

Chapter Three

Music Hall and Vaudeville

MUSIC HALL

Music hall lies at the root of all modern popular entertainment. At the beginning of the 19th Century people sang traditional songs in taverns and customers staged their own performances. Food and drink were served and special rooms set aside for the entertainment. These places were known as free-and-easies. There was no charge for admission but refreshments were supplied at the usual rates. There was a chairman, who was usually a good singer himself, and a pianist. Any amateur could sing or perform if they gave their name to the chairman. These free-and-easies were happy-go-lucky places that gave mainly young male amateurs a chance to perform.

Many historians attribute the rise of music hall to the Theatre Regulation Act of 1843. This legislation finally abolished the Patent Monopoly, thus any type of theatre could apply for a Lord Chamberlain's Licence to present drama. Taverns and inns offering entertainment and serving food and drink were subject to a magistrate's licence, but were not permitted to put on drama. This dual licensing system meant that music hall and theatre developed separately but there were occasions when problems occurred as late as 1911, when the newly opened Palladium in London was fined for allowing an excerpt of *Julius Caesar*.

After 1843 music halls were usually built as an extension to a tavern or Public House. The first purpose-built music hall was The Canterbury, situated in Westminster Bridge Road in London. In 1849 Charles Morton took over the hall that had a room in which free-and-easies were staged. He refurbished and improved the room and in 1851 obtained a music licence. Professional performers were engaged and the amateur element of music hall came to an end.

A new building was opened in 1852 and Morton engaged Sam Cowell, whose most popular song was 'Lord Lovell'. He was possibly the first music hall star. He began his career at the age of nine in America but in 1840 achieved success at the Edinburgh Adelphi. In the late 1840s he decided to concentrate on character singing and rose to the top of his profession. He toured extensively in England and embarked on a tour of America and Canada in 1860. Alcohol and over-work led to his death on his return to England. His last performance was in 1861, preceding his death in 1864.

The first generation of music hall artists are nowadays remembered mostly by the songs that they made famous and these were often sung in a unique style.

Harry Clifton (1832–72) His songs fell into three categories; comic, Irish and 'motto songs', which had a strong moral tone to them. Some of his best-known songs are 'Polly Perkins of Paddington Green' and 'A Dark Girl Dressed in Blue'. His most well-remembered 'motto songs' are 'Paddle Your Own Canoe' and 'Tramp, Tramp, Tramp, the Boys are Marching', sung to the music of the marching song of the American Civil War.

Sam Collins (1827–65) A popular singer of the 1840s who specialised in Irish songs such as 'The Rocky Road to Dublin'. He was very successful and in November 1863 opened Sam Collins Music Hall in Islington. Later known as Collins Music Hall, it remained in use until it was damaged by fire in 1958. Sir Norman Wisdom made his professional debut there in 1945.

Frederick Robson (1821–64) He had many successes as a comic singer in the music halls and also the theatre, creating roles such as Jem Baggs in *The Wandering Minstrel*. 'Vilikens and his Dinah' was one of his most famous songs.

J.H. Stead (1827–86) He made his name with one song, 'The Perfect Cure', which he sang dressed as a French curate.

However, more remarkable was the strange jumping dance he performed, without bending his knees, at the end of each chorus.

Sam Cowell and his contemporaries often appeared on stage looking down-at-heel. The next group of music hall artists chose to play the fop, the swell, the dandy, and the well-dressed man-about-town.

George Laybourne (1842–84) His most popular songs remembered and performed to this day are 'Champagne Charlie' and 'The Daring Young Man on the Flying Trapeze'.

Arthur Lloyd (1839–1904) Wrote many successful songs including 'The Song of Songs', 'Not for Joe' and 'The German Band'.

G.H. MacDermott (1845–1901) Modelled himself on Alfred Vance but was not only a music hall artist but also an actor, playwright, and theatre proprietor. 'The Scamp', a slightly risqué song, 'Dear Old Pals' and 'The War Song', a patriotic number, are among his most well-remembered songs. The latter caused a sensation when it was first sung in 1877 and visitors to London, many of whom had never visited a music hall, crowded to see MacDermott perform the song at the London Pavilion.

Alfred Vance (1839–88) Made his Music Hall debut in 1864. His best remembered songs are 'Walking the Zoo', the motto song, 'Act on the Square' and 'Clicquot', extolling champagne.

A year after George Laybourne's death in 1884 the three great entertainers of the music hall emerged. They were Marie Lloyd (1870–1922), Dan Leno (1860–1904) and Little Tich (1867–1928).

Marie Lloyd was a star at the age of 20 and remained so until her death 32 years later. She sang a wide range of character songs that changed as she grew older and saucy songs, made even saucier by a wink, a naughty look, or a movement of her dress. She was a generous and big-hearted woman who appealed to both royalty and the ordinary man, although she was unlucky in love and had three failed marriages. She made five trips to America and one to Australia and was a highly paid performer. Her first success in 1885 was 'The Boy in the Gallery', originally sung by Nellie Power. There were many other successes such as 'Oh Mr Porter' (1892), 'Don't Dilly Dally' (1917) and 'A Little of What You Fancy' (1915). This last song typifies her style. As well as performing in music hall, she also appeared in pantomime for several years at Drury Lane with Dan Leno. Her last years were affected by poor health and she died three days after collapsing following a performance at the Edmonton Empire in October 1922. As many as 50,000 people lined the funeral route, demonstrating the affection directed towards this music hall star. There are several recordings made by Marie Lloyd that capture her vitality and comic timing.

Dan Leno first performed at the age of four and appeared with his brother at the age of six in a dancing double act. When Dan was eight he made his solo debut at The Britannia, Hoxton. During his teenage years he toured with his family, performing solo song and dance acts. He made his first adult appearance in London in 1885. He developed a comic style that became a legend in his lifetime, playing a wide range of characters; the railway guard, the detective, the county councillor, the holiday-maker and many more. His songs were less important than the comic patter that was part of them, which he developed in his own unique style. He first appeared in pantomime in 1886 as Dame Durden in Jack and the Beanstalk and is remembered as one of the great pantomime dames, appearing at Drury Lane many times.

Dan made one visit to America in 1897, which was not entirely successful. Towards the end of his life he became unstable and he died in 1904. He is remembered for his genius and loveable personality. As with Marie Lloyd, thousands of people followed his funeral. Max Beerbohm wrote:

'I defy anyone not to have loved Dan Leno at first sight. The moment he capered on (the stage) with that air of wild determination, squirming in every limb with some deep grievance that must be outpoured, all hearts were his.'

'The Huntsman', performed before King Edward VII and Queen Alexandra, 'The Doctor' and 'The May Day Fireman' are just some of Dan Leno's songs.

Little Tich's Big Boot dance became famous throughout Europe and America. He was born in Kent and only grew to 4ft 6in in height. He spent his early years performing 'funny dances' and comic songs at local free-and-easies. In 1884 he made his London debut at the Marylebone and the Foresters Music Hall. Two trips to America followed where he was very successful; his act was very visual and appealed to this audience. On his return in 1890 he appeared in pantomime with Marie Lloyd and Dan Leno in *Humpty Dumpty* at the Drury Lane Theatre. He realised that comic dancing was an international act and appeared extensively in Europe with particularly good success in Paris. His act remained almost the same for many years, a song, some patter and a dance in character. 'I'm an Inspector' (1895) was one of his most successful character songs but there were many more, such as 'The Dentist', 'The Toreador' and 'The Zoo Keeper'. He made many recordings of his songs between 1911 and 1917 so we are able to appreciate some idea of his style. During an engagement at the Alhambra in 1927 he introduced a new character to his act, the charlady at the House of Commons. Unfortunately an accident with his prop mop caused him to knock his head and he shortly afterwards suffered a stroke and never spoke again. He died three months later.

At the turn of the century there were music halls in all big towns in England and Scotland, but London was the mecca of this style of theatre and entertainment. Frank Matcham was the most famous architect of both music halls and legitimate theatres, being responsible for about 150 buildings. They were very elaborate in design and decor, however few remain; many were destroyed in the 1960s. In fact, of the 1,100 British theatres standing in 1914, 85 percent had been lost or irretrievably altered by 1980. In 2004 the London Coliseum and the Hackney Empire were reopened, having been restored to their former glory so that today's audience can now appreciate Frank Matcham's architecture. The Players Theatre in Villiers Street off the Strand was the last theatre in the world offering a modern representation of Victorian music hall. Sadly it closed in 2002.

Music hall performers were identified or associated with their own particular songs, and in many cases the composers and writers received little credit. Examples are as follows:

Albert Chevalier (1861–1923) 'Wot cher (Knocked 'em in the Old Kent Road)' (1891) and 'My Old Dutch' (1892) ('Old Dutch' or 'Duchess of Fife' is cockney rhyming slang for wife).

Eugene Stratton (1861–1918) 'Little Dolly Daydream' (1897) and 'Lily of Laguna' (1898).

The two most popular Scottish performers were:

Will Fyffe (1885–1947) 'I belong to Glasgow' (1921).

Harry Lauder (1870–1950) 'I Love a Lassie' (1905), 'Stop Yer Tickling, Jock' (1904), 'A Wee Deoch-and-Doris' (1910) and 'Keep Right on to the End of the Road' (1924).

Both of these artists achieved success in the halls but during their long careers they performed in films and variety and also recorded many of their popular songs.

There were many female music hall stars apart from Marie Lloyd. Many achieved success as male impersonators such as:

Hetty King (1883–1972) 'Ship Ahoy' (1909).

Ella Shields (1879–1952) 'Burlington Bertie from Bow' (1914).

Vesta Tilly (1864–1952); 'After the Ball' (1893), 'Following in Father's Footsteps' (1902) and 'Jolly Good Luck to the Girl Who Loves a Soldier' (1906).

These artists appeared both in Britain and America and they had long and distinguished careers.

The Australian artist Florrie Ford (1875–1940) had a long career both in her native Australia and in Britain. She performed, amongst others, 'Down at the Old Bull and Bush' (1903), 'Oh! Oh! Antonio' (1908) and 'Has Anybody Here Seen Kelly' (1909). She made her debut in London in 1897 and was particularly successful in encouraging the audience to sing along with her, which they usually did with great gusto. During her long career she was very generous and gave away a great deal of her money. When she died, Louis MacNeice wrote a tribute poem to her called 'Death of an Actress'.

In the early days of music hall (1866–70) the chairman was very important as he had a commanding presence and controlled the rowdy element of the audience. He relied on a vivid use of language, using exaggerated alliteration to introduce the different artists. From 1953 BBC Television ran a series called *The Good Old Days*, filmed from the City of Variety, Leeds, with Leonard Sachs as the chairman and a live audience dressed in Edwardian clothes. The programme ran for 30 years and performers recreated the songs of past music hall stars and comedians. The following artists were associated with songs that are remembered to this day.

Harry Champion (1886–1942) 'Boiled Beef and Carrots', 'I'm Henery the Eighth I Am' and 'Any Old Iron'.

Charles Coborn (1852–1945) 'Two Lovely Black Eyes' and 'The Man Who Broke the Bank at Monte Carlo'.

Gus Ellen (1862–1940) 'If it Wasn't For the Houses in Between' and 'It's a Great Big Shame'.

Billy Merson (1881–1947) 'The Spaniard That Blighted My Life'.

Albert Whelan (1875–1961) 'The Preacher and the Bear'.

There were some artists who were 'one hit wonders' only, although they performed for many years and a few of these are as follows.

Lotty Collins (1865–1910) 'Ta-ra-ra-boom-de-ay'.

Leo Dryden (1863–1939) 'The Miners Dream of Home'.

Randolph Sutton (1888–1969) 'On Mother Kelly's Doorstep'.

There is an interesting anecdote in which Randolph Sutton, towards the end of his lifetime, had heard that 'his song' was being sung by a young female impersonator. Randolph was not impressed. However, chance was to bring them together at a 'Water Rats' dinner. They talked together and an instant rapport was established, culminating in Randolph giving a youthful Danny La Rue his personal endorsement to continue singing 'his song' – 'On Mother Kelly's Doorstep'.

Don Ross, music hall's last impresario, staged a re-creation using artists still working in the genre but through the outlet of variety theatre. This was called *Thanks for the Memory*. In December 1950 the final performance of this show was given at the Empress, Brixton, and recorded by the BBC. In 2004 a CD of the show was released featuring Randolph Sutton, Nellie Wallace, Ella Shields, Talbot O'Farrel, Gertie Gitana, Billy Danvers and G.H. Elliott.

During the late 1800s many successful music hall artists crossed the Atlantic to appear in American vaudeville. Tony Pastor, who started out as a performer himself at the age of six, later entered management. In 1865 he opened Tony Pastor's Opera House in New York and later leased many other theatres. He booked many British artists to appear in his theatres:

Annie Adams (1843–1905) made a two-year tour of America between 1871 and 1873 and was paid a fortune. Other artists, encouraged by her success, visited New York and other major cities.

Jenny Hill (1850–96) travelled to New York in 1890 and was paid £150 per week (£900 by today's standards). 'I've Been a

Good Woman to You' and 'Sweet Violets' were among some of her famous songs.

Vesta Victoria (1873–1951) first went to America in 1893 and in time became equally famous in both Britain and America. 'Daddy Wouldn't Buy Me a Bow-Wow' and 'Waiting at the Church' were two of her hit songs.

Alice Lloyd (1873–1949), sister to Marie, achieved great success in America. She made her debut in the country in 1907 and the Brooklyn Daily Eagle reported:

> *'Miss Lloyd is of the pink and white, Dresden china type and renders her songs in a dainty, modest and demure manner, instead of hurling them at her audience as we have come to expect from English singers.'*

Music hall went into gradual decline after World War I. Audiences and society had changed and other forms of entertainment were preferred such as cinema, ragtime, revue and radio. Music hall theatres became cinemas and in 1929 the first talking pictures were screened. However, the tradition of music hall is still alive and the songs are still sung in London pubs. The public's fondness for nostalgia ensures that this form of entertainment will never really die.

VAUDEVILLE

Vaudeville is predominately an American style of variety entertainment that flourished from the middle of the 19th Century until the early part of the 20th Century. It developed from many sources, including shows in saloons, pantomime, minstrel and freak shows.

It differed from British music hall in that there was no chairman and food and drink were not available. There was always a great variety of acts on the bill. A typical programme would include singers, dancers, comedians and various speciality acts including circus performers, animal acts, mind readers, escape artists, balancing acts and contortionists. Celebrities from other fields, such as Helen Keller and the movie star Douglas Fairbanks, would make personal appearances, receiving thousands of dollars.

The origins of the term 'vaudeville' are unclear. Some suggest the word is a corruption of the French term 'voix de ville', a slang term meaning songs of the town. Others say it came from 'veaux de vire', a valley in Normandy noted for its satirical and topical songs. However, by the 1880s vaudeville was established as a form of entertainment that bridged the social classes. On October 21st 1881 Tony Pastor, a devout catholic and family man, presented his first 'clean' variety bill at New York's Fourteenth Street Theater. Each week Pastor offered a different line-up of quality acts that drew an enthusiastic audience of all age groups and classes, including some of the most influential people of New York.

Vaudeville spread throughout America and major theatre chains or circuits were built. Artists were booked to tour for several weeks at a time, sometimes even years. A successful act toured for 40 weeks or more each year and made good money. More than 25,000 people performed in vaudeville over the years of its existence.

Benjamin Franklin Keith founded the most important circuit of theatres. His first theatre was The Bijou Theater in Boston, Massachusetts, and here he developed the policy of continuous performance. The performance ran for up to 12 hours and scheduled acts would appear two or three times. The theatres appeared to be always busy and this encouraged the audience to enter the theatre as they were reassured by numbers. Keith's idea revolutionised variety entertainment and the length of the performances opened vaudeville to wider audiences. Edward F. Albee became manager of the Keith circuit and together they became the most successful team in vaudeville. They were committed to 'polite' entertainment and any acts that used suggestive words or offensive language were not allowed to continue their engagement. Sophie Tucker, a famous vaudeville performer explains in her autobiography how Keith's theatre managers assessed every act during the first performance of the week's engagement:

> *'Between the matinee and the night show the blue envelopes began to appear in the performers' mailboxes backstage... Inside would be a curt order to cut out a blue line of a song, or piece of business. Sometimes there was a suggestion of something you could substitute for the material the manager ordered out... There was no arguing about the orders in the blue envelopes. They were final. You obeyed them or quit. And if you quit, you got a black mark against your name in the head office and you didn't work on the Keith Circuit any more.'*

Some of These Days by Sophie Tucker

Nowadays anything risqué has become known as 'blue material' because of the colour of the envelopes.

There were three levels of performers as defined by the trade newspaper, Variety:

Small time – small town and cheaper theatres in large towns. Performers made as little as $15 a week in the early years and later nearer to $75. Often these dates were a training ground for new performers or old-timers at the end of their careers.

Medium time – good theatres in a wide range of cities, offering salaries of up to a few hundred dollars a week. Performers seen here were either on their way up or on their way down.

Big time – the finest theatres in a wide range of cities, using a two performance-a-day format. Most big time acts earned hundreds of dollars per week, and headliners could command $1000 a week, sometimes even more.

A vaudeville act could be almost anything that was inoffensive and entertaining. Performers could be any gender, race or appearance as long as they gave an audience 10 to 15 minutes of diversion. Singers and dancers were part of every bill, but it was the speciality acts that made vaudeville unique.

A typical bill followed the basic format:

1   The opening was a silent act that would not be ruined by the audience settling into their seats – acrobats or animal acts were ideal. Any other kind being booked in the spot was the ultimate insult.

2   Usually a double act, singing or dancing. The youngest member of the Gumm Sisters went on to fame after changing her name to Judy Garland.

3   A comedy sketch or one-act play. These were often melodramas with unknown casts or new plays featuring Broadway stars such as Sarah Bernhart, Ethel Barrymore and Helen Hayes. Some of the finest writers provided sketches and one-act plays for vaudeville including J.M. Barrie, Sir Arthur Conan Doyle and W.S. Gilbert.

4   A novelty act or eccentric dance to liven things up.

5   This spot was reserved for rising stars or falling ones to close the first half of the programme on a high note.

6   After the interval came a big act involving a large set – choirs, orchestras or top animal acts.

7   'Next-to-closing' was the star spot reserved for headliners – usually a vocalist or comedian. Stars such as Jack Benny, Sophie Tucker and Al Jolson were among some of the headliners that appeared in vaudeville.

8   The closing spot was reserved for short films or annoying acts that might encourage the audience to leave before the next show.

The most celebrated vaudeville theatre in the early 1900s was New York's Victoria on 42nd Street. The Orpheum Circuit had well-appointed houses across the western United States. The Palace Theater, built by Martin Beck, was soon taken over by Keith and Albee who now ran the largest and most successful circuit of vaudeville theatres throughout America. Top managers and theatrical agents packed the Monday matinees at the Palace, so a successful performance there would lead to good bookings nationwide.

Many words and sayings that have become part of theatre language owe their origins to vaudeville. To give conductors the proper tempo, dancers would beat their feet on the stage before entering. The resulting sound, like a horse pounding its hooves, led to the still-popular nickname of 'hoofer' for a dancer.

Top stars or headliners keen to protect their expensive costumes had bright red carpet laid between their dressing rooms and the stage, thus the term 'the red carpet treatment'.

If a performer received a very good response from the audience the following artist had to work twice as hard, thus you were a 'hard act to follow'.

By the mid 1920s the public's tastes changed and vaudeville's managers and most of the performers failed to adjust to the changes. Just as in Britain, where music hall slowly died as a popular form of entertainment, in America vaudeville lost its audience to films. In 1928 Albee went into partnership with Joseph P. Kennedy's Hollywood film company to form Radio Keith Orpheum (RKO) Studios and the theatres of the celebrated circuit became cinemas. In the 1930s talking films and the Great Depression finally wiped away the last vestiges of vaudeville.

However, the influence of vaudeville can still be found in some of the popular musicals of today. Chicago, with music by Kander and Ebb, is based on many popular vaudeville acts and various performers, thus keeping alive this traditional form of entertainment.

DISCUSSION POINTS

• *Where does music hall have its origins?*

• *Choose three well-known music hall artists and give a brief outline of their careers and the songs which made them famous.*

• *What do you know about the role of 'chairman' in a music hall performance?*

MUSIC HALL AND VAUDEVILLE

- *What is the difference between music hall and vaudeville?*

- *Where does vaudeville have its origins and who was the key person in its development?*

- *Describe a typical vaudeville entertainment.*

REFERENCES

Baker, Richard Anthony – *British Music Hall: An Illustrated History* Sutton Publishing, 2005

Bratton, Jacqueline S. – *Music Hall: Performance and Style* Open University Press, 1986

Davison, Peter – *Songs of the British Music Hall* Music Sales Ltd, 1971

Gillies, Midge – *Marie Lloyd: The One and Only* Wiedenfeld and Nicolson, 1999

Honri, Peter – *Music Hall Warriors* Greenwich Exchange, 1997

Hudd, Roy – *Roy Hudd's Cavalcade of Variety Acts, 1945–60* Robson Books Ltd, 1998

www.musicals101.com

Chapter Four

Jazz Musicals

The task confronting a writer who undertakes to describe, define and categorise jazz and from that, the place of jazz in musicals, is a challenging one. The problem with defining jazz is that it eludes definition, as throughout its comparatively brief history jazz has been, by and large, played and written intuitively. This isn't to say, however, that it is an unstructured form or that, however informal its origins, an unsophisticated one.

So the challenge begins!

BACKGROUND AND HISTORICAL/MUSICAL CONTEXT

It is generally accepted that jazz developed towards the latter part of the 19th Century from black work songs, field hollers or shouts, sorrow songs, hymns and spirituals whose harmonic, melodic and rhythmic components were predominantly African. It may be argued that due to its emotional, spontaneous and often improvisational nature, and because of its black origins, jazz has, to some extent, never been accorded the true degree of recognition it deserves.

Jazz is generally thought to have begun in New Orleans, spreading to Chicago, Kansas City, New York City and finally the West Coast. The blues, both vocal and instrumental, are a vital component of jazz, which in a rough order of appearance would include ragtime, New Orleans or Dixieland jazz, swing, bop or bebop, progressive or cool jazz, neo-bop or hard bop, third stream, mainstream modern, Latin-jazz, jazz rock and avant-garde or free jazz.

Jazz uses blue notes, swing, syncopation, call and response, polyrhythms and improvisation, blending African-

American musical styles with Western music techniques and theories.

Many have argued that the 'non-jazz' elements from which jazz was formed (the blues, ragtime, brass band music, hymns and Spirituals etc) were ubiquitous and to be found everywhere in the United States. Why then is New Orleans singled out as the birthplace of jazz? The underlying factor must be, perhaps, one that existed in New Orleans only, namely the black Creole subculture.

The Creoles were free, French and Spanish-speaking Blacks, originally from the West Indies. The Creole musicians, many of whom were conservatoire-trained, prided themselves in their formal knowledge of European music and techniques. In contrast were the musicians of the American (or back o' town) section schooled in the blues, Gospel music and work songs which were sung or played mostly by ear. Use of memory and improvisation were the characteristics of the west-side bands; sight reading and correct performance were the characteristics of Creole bands. It was, perhaps, the musical sparks that flew on the meeting of these very different cultures, during the next decade, which sparked the flames of jazz!

Jelly Roll (a Creole named Ferdinand La Menthe at birth) was undoubtedly a predominant force in the early development of jazz. It can be argued that he isolated a music not yet covered by the blues or ragtime. He applied a swinging syncopation to a variety of music, including ragtime, opera and both French and Spanish songs and dances. He may also have introduced the 2-bar break (the forerunner of extended solos), scat singing and other improvisational ideas. So the conversion of ragtime to jazz began; this involved applying a strong underlying 4/4 beat (four to the bar) to 2/4 ragtime. With this evolvement any music from opera to the blues could be 'played hot' as it was described in those early days.

So we can see that both African and European rhythms were being employed. African music supplied the strong underlined beat, the use of polyrhythms and the idea of a melody being played separate from or 'above' the beat. European music, meanwhile, provided more formal dance rhythms. Combined, these rhythms give jazz its characteristic swing.

It has been said that jazz is the art of expression set to music. Those who play and sing it have often expressed the opinion that jazz should remain undefined, that it should be 'felt'. As Louis Armstrong (1900–71), the unique and hugely influential genius who was not only a brilliant musician of incalculable influence but perhaps the first great 'ground breaker' of jazz, put it: 'If you gotta ask, you'll never know.'

JAZZ SINGING AND JAZZ PLAYING

The first singers in jazz were not really jazz singers; they were pop singers who sang the blues, sometimes accompanied by jazz musicians. Here we have to address a very important issue in the relationship between jazz singing and playing. Jazz singing does not bear the same relationship to other types of singing that jazz playing does to other kinds of instrumental music. Jazz singing has to be defined differently from jazz playing.

It has been put forward by some that the only true jazz singers are those who use their voices like an instrument; for example, introducing the theme (with or without words) and then building an improvisation (nearly always wordless) on the theme, just as a saxophonist or pianist would do. However, the human voice simply doesn't have the flexibility that other instruments do. Also, in a good song, words and music are intricately and inextricably mixed in a unique way. The singer of jazz is therefore tied more firmly, perhaps, to his or her source material (their original song or theme) than the jazz instrumentalist. As a result, jazz singing has had to develop its own rules, its own basis of improvisation, indeed its own 'jazzness'. The jazz singer, therefore, potentially improvises, not just on a theme or line, but on each part of a line, word or syllable. This movement, shaping and re-shaping, affects both the music and the sense of the word or words.

A BRIEF GLOSSARY OF MUSICAL TERMS RELATING TO JAZZ SINGING AND PERFORMANCE RATHER THAN PLAYING:

Blue note – *A slight flattening of the third, fifth or seventh note of the major scale for expressive effect.*

Blues – *An improvised genre for solo voice, often accompanied by a solo instrument such as a guitar in a 'call and response' pattern, which exerted a major influence on the development of jazz.*

Call and response – *A musical 'question and answer' pattern where a theme is passed rapidly from one performer, or group, to another. Probably derived from antiphonal singing common in slave working parties.*

Field holler – *A work song (or shout) originated by slaves on plantations.*

Hot – *A term popular in early jazz, referring to parts of a performance which sound 'jazzy' eg swung rhythm, syncopation and blue notes.*

Improvisation – *The spontaneous production of musical ideas by a performer, involving no conscious element of pre-composition.*

Meter – *The organisation of rhythmic pulses into regular stress patterns.*

Scat singing – *Singing an improvised melodic line to nonsense syllables, often in imitation of instrumental music.*

Spiritual – *Vocal music of the black American church.*

Swung rhythm – *The tendency of jazz performers to anticipate the main beats of a meter through syncopation, or by altering notes of long and short rhythmic values. The techniques move the music forward with a strong rhythmic drive.*

Symphonic jazz – *A hybrid style combining elements of both jazz and classical music. Gershwin, among others, popularised this in the 1920s and '30s.*

Syncopation – *Accenting the weak beat to disrupt the expected stress pattern in a regular meter.*

Vaudeville – *A staged variety show, popular in America at the turn of the 20th Century (broadly comparable to the music hall tradition in Britain). Its musical content was important to the early development of jazz.*

A JAZZ POT-POURRI SELECTION

There follows a pot-pourri of songs, background details, musical contexts and anecdotes in order to capture the style, diversity, appeal and universal influence of jazz in song and musical theatre.

'Alexander's Ragtime Band' (1911) by Irving Berlin was his first major hit. The lyrics clearly refer to the arrival of African American musicians onto the popular scene with their 'new' idea of playing standard songs in a more exciting up-tempo style ('Jazzing up'). The song has been recorded by many artists including Al Jolson, Louis Armstrong, George Formby, Bing Crosby, Ella Fitzgerald and Ray Charles. A 1938 film of the same name was loosely based on the song.

'Chicago' (1922) by Fred Fisher. It was originally a vaudeville hit for Blossom Seeley, later recorded by Frank Sinatra in 1957.

'It Had To Be You' (1924) by Isham Jones and Gus Kahn. It was performed by Priscilla Lane in the 1939 film *The Roaring Twenties*, by Dooley Wilson in the 1942 film *Casablanca* and by Diane Keaton in the 1977 film *Annie Hall*.

'Fascinating Rhythm' (1924) by George and Ira Gershwin. This hugely popular song was first introduced by Fred Astaire and his sister, Adele, in the Broadway musical *Lady Be Good*. The Astaires also recorded the song in 1926 with George Gershwin on the piano. A large number of versions exist. One of the rarest recordings is by Joe Bari (a pseudonym of Anthony Dominick Bernedetto), who is better known as Tony Bennett.

'Someone To Watch Over Me' (1926) by George and Ira Gershwin from the musical *O, Kay!* It was also performed by, amongst others, Frank Sinatra, Perry Como, Ella Fitzgerald and Linda Ronstadt. It has become a jazz standard and a key work in the Great American Songbook.

'Can't Help Lovin' Dat Man' (1927) by Jerome Kern and Oscar Hammerstein II is one of the most famous songs from their classic musical play, *Show Boat*, adapted from Edna Ferber's novel. The song is written in a blues tempo and is sung by several characters in the show, but is most closely associated with the mixed-raced character, Julie.

'Ain't Misbehavin'' is a musical revue, with a book by Murray Horwitz and Richard Maltby Jr and music by Thomas Wright 'Fats' Waller. It takes its title from the 1929 Waller song, 'Ain't Misbehavin''. It is a tribute to the black musicians of the 1920s and '30s who were part of the Harlem Renaissance, an era of creativity, cultural awareness and ethnic pride.

'I Got Rhythm' (1930) by George Gershwin from *Girl Crazy*. The song has been recorded by a number of performers including Judy Garland and Ethel Waters. It also featured in the 1951 film, *An American in Paris*, starring Gene Kelly.

'It Don't Mean a Thing (if it Ain't Got That Swing)' (1932) is a composition by Duke Ellington and Irving Mills. It is now accepted as a jazz standard.

'Stormy Weather' (1933) is a song written by Harold Arlen and Ted Koehler. Ethel Waters first sang it at The Cotton Club nightclub in Harlem. In 2004 it was one of 50 recordings chosen by the Library of Congress to be added to the National Recording Registry. Lena Horne became famous in 1943 for her rendition of 'Stormy Weather' in the film of the same name.

'I Get a Kick Out of You' is a song by Cole Porter, originally featured in *Anything Goes* (1934). Originally sung by Ethel

Merman, it has been covered by many performers including Louis Armstrong, Rosemary Clooney, Jamie Cullum, Ella Fitzgerald, Billie Holiday, Dolly Parton, Frank Sinatra and Dinah Washington.

'Summertime' by George and Ira Gershwin and DuBose Heyward is a classic jazz standard from the musical opera *Porgy and Bess* (1935).

'My Funny Valentine' by Richard Rogers and Lorenz Hart first appeared in the musical comedy *Babes in Arms* (1937). It is now a jazz standard appearing on over 1300 albums and performed by over 600 artists. The song re-emerged in the 1950s and has been performed by many great jazz musicians and vocalists including Frank Sinatra, Ella Fitzgerald, Sarah Vaughan, Tony Bennett and Buddy Rich to name but a few.

'Bewitched, Bothered and Bewildered' (1940) from the stage musical *Pal Joey*. This became a film in 1957 featuring Frank Sinatra and Rita Hayworth. The song was rediscovered in the 1950s and no less than seven different versions reached the top of the US charts.

'Beat Out Dat Rhythm on a Drum' from the Broadway musical *Carmen Jones* (1943). This was an updating of Bizet's opera, *Carmen*, in an African-American setting. Many of the show's songs retain a surprising impact to the present day. The feverish intensity of 'Beat Out...' hasn't lessened and the song has been covered by a wide variety of performers from Pearl Bailey to Marc Almond.

'The Rhythm of Life' from the musical *Sweet Charity* (1966) by Cy Coleman and Dorothy Fields (book by Neil Simon). The original production ran for 608 performances and was nominated for 12 Tony Awards. The 1969 film version featured Sammy Davis Jr. whose character memorably sang the song.

'All That Jazz' is the opening number from *Chicago* (1975) by John Kander and Fred Ebb, two of musical theatre's unsung giants. Chicago returned to both Broadway and the West End in the late 1990s to a most enthusiastic reception and to far greater success than its debut. The score of *Chicago* evokes the American jazz scene of the 1920s.

ESSENTIALLY JAZZ...ESSENTIALLY GERSHWIN

George Gershwin (1898–1937) was undoubtedly one of the most gifted musicians ever. As a 16 year old, when discussing jazz with his teacher, he is reported to have said,

> *'This is American music. This is the kind of music I want to write.'*

Gershwin took the three ingredients that went into the folk songs of the streets of New York – jazz, ragtime and the blues – and out of these he wove a characteristic popular art. He was deeply affected by the syncopated rhythms and forceful energy of jazz which was at that point a new, vibrant and wonderfully subversive element in the world of music.

His first hit, 'Swanee', was brought to fame by Al Jolson. He had an astonishing gift for spontaneous melody. In his many and memorable show tunes we can see a profile of his distinctive style: fresh lyricism, subtle rhythms (sometimes caressing, then driving), chromatic harmony and sudden modulation.

Even to this day Gershwin's songs have tremendous staying power. His music is popular, not only among jazz and Broadway performers, but universally. Gershwin was a master of many styles; consider the range from 'Swanee' to 'I Got Rhythm' to 'Rhapsody in Blue'.

PORGY AND BESS: PAST, PRESENT AND INTO THE FUTURE

Stephen Sondheim reportedly considers *Porgy and Bess* to be

> *'the only musical that will last, that will seem great, one hundred years from now.'*

It was, perhaps, far-and-away Gershwin's most ambitious creation. Having come across DuBose Hayward's novel,

Porgy, in 1926, Gershwin recognised it immediately as an ideal vehicle for a folk opera, using blues and jazz idioms.

In the autumn of 1935 the completed work, which ran for four hours, was performed in a concert version at Carnegie Hall. Over the years various versions have been presented worldwide and it has now come to be regarded as one of the great operas of the 20th Century.

Many of its songs are now considered timeless classics, such as 'It Ain't Necessarily So', 'I Got Plenty of Nuttin', 'I Loves You, Porgy' and what has now become a jazz standard, 'Summertime'.

George Gershwin was passionate about his work reaching the widest possible audience. He understood that adaptation was a part of keeping his work 'alive' in order, as he said, 'To appeal to the many rather than the cultured few'.

Taking him at his word, Trevor Nunn's 2007 London production has evolved as a result of his going back to all available sources: the original novel, the play and the libretto. He has developed a version of the piece that, in vocal range and structure, has the quality of musical theatre rather than of opera.

It is reported that Gershwin originally intended his work to have a jazz prologue. This was a thrilling piece of music cut from the score before the original opening. A similar fate happened to the character Maria's devastating 'Rap Song' attack on the sleazy character, Sporting Life. The London production reinstated both of these with great success.

IN CONCLUSION...

Gershwin took the ingredients of jazz, ragtime and the blues (to which, in *Porgy and Bess*, he added the Negro spiritual). His aim was to reconcile jazz and classical, or as was said in those days, 'to bring Tin Pan Alley to Carnegie Hall'.

To Gershwin, jazz was a natural mode of expression through which he showed to the world the charm of popular music. A charm which, with the help of his and others genius, will continue to enjoy universal appeal into the future.

Long Live Musical Theatre! Long Live Jazz!

DISCUSSION POINTS

- *What are the problems when defining jazz?*

- *How did jazz develop?*

- *What do you know about jazz singing and how does it differ from other styles of singing?*

- *What do you know about George Gershwin and what role did he play in the development of jazz musicals?*

- *Which musical by Kander and Ebb evokes the American jazz scene of the 1920s and its links to vaudeville? What do you know about it?*

- *Many jazz songs are lifted from their original musicals and recorded separately by well known jazz artistes, with great success. Can you give any examples of this?*

REFERENCES

Berendt, Joachim E., *The Story of Jazz* Barrie & Jenkins, 1978

Berendt, Joachim E., *The Jazz Book: From Ragtime to Fusion and Beyond* A Capella Books, 2002

Cooke, Mervyn, *The Chronicle of Jazz* Abbeville Press Inc., 1998

Chapter Five

Book Musicals

THE BOOK MUSICAL

The musical is most definitely an art form. In the best book musical, a play or novel combines with songs, dance and stagecraft to create the artistic entity. The most successful are collaborations between composer, lyricist, producer, director, choreographer, costume and lighting designers, orchestrator, actors and many more.

The book musical is perhaps the most common type of musical in the West End and on Broadway, made up of a narrative libretto (Italian: meaning 'little book') providing the plot. To be a book musical, it must have either an introduction, development and conclusion, or a beginning, middle and end, so showing the progression of time. Other types of musical tend to show distortions within the storyline.

The book refers to the written word – the play or story of the show: the spoken lines. In most true book musicals the story has been adapted from an already published book or play, such as Rudyard Kipling's *The Jungle Book*. The lyrics of the songs must be part of the storyline and help to develop the plot. The music and lyrics together form the score.

It is very difficult to clearly define which musicals should take the title of a book musical, a light opera or an operetta, as some have received both musical theatre and operatic treatment. Similarly, some older operettas or light operas have had modern productions or adaptations that treated them very much as musicals. Sondheim said:

'I really think that when something plays Broadway it's a musical, and when it plays in an opera house it's opera. That's it. It's the terrain, the countryside, the expectations of the audience that make it one thing or another.'

There will always be some overlap between lighter operatic forms and the more musically complex or ambitious musicals, but it is the style of the song within the musical/operetta that will define the genre.

The book musical should tell a story, and like most good stories, it should have its moments of tension and drama. The composer and librettist work closely together to compose and write songs that suit the character and their situation, reflecting these emotional heights in song. The song should develop naturally from the performers' understanding and emotional belief in the character and the world around them.

THE HISTORY

When was the first book musical written? It is difficult to define its beginnings, for many different types of musical theatre forms influenced and transformed what we now call 'the musical', as discussed earlier.

In 1926 Edna Ferber wrote her best-selling novel, *Show Boat*, and within 12 months the composer, Jerome Kern, and lyricist-librettist, Oscar Hammerstein II, produced one of the most powerful and popular musicals ever written. The story traces the lives of a Mississippi riverboat family, their troupe of actors and deck crew through several generations; dealing with racism and marital heartbreak. This wonderful story came to life with songs that were hits then and that we still all know and love today – 'Make Believe', 'Old Man River' and 'You Are Love'. This is the first true book musical. Even here we can see the influence of the early minstrel stories.

The Revue was very popular in Britain in the 1920s and '30s, but it was from this genre that a British newcomer, whose talents as an actor, playwright, composer and lyricist would make him the brightest light in the British theatre, arose. Noel Coward conquered both London and America with his songs and plays. His operetta, *Bitter Sweet* (1929), was the only British book musical imported to Broadway in the 1920s.

Bitter Sweet does bridge the two genres of operetta and the book musical.

One of the longest running Broadway book musicals of the 1930s was George and Ira Gershwin's *Of Thee I Sing* (1931). The Gershwins worked with script writers George S. Kaufman and Morrie Ryskind on this satirical tale of a President who gets elected because he marries the woman he loves. Several scenes were set to music in a semi-operatic format, but the score was pure musical comedy. *Of Thee I Sing* was the first musical ever to win the Pulitzer Prize for drama.

DuBose Heyward's play, *Porgy and Bess*, was adapted by the Gershwins into a very well-known jazz opera which, although it fits into the book musical category, offers a blend of classical, popular and jazz styles. The story is about the struggle and poverty of a black African American family living in the tenements of Charleston's Catfish Row, South Carolina. The community focuses on its general despair and the violent nature of life there.

The longest running West End book musical from this period was *Me and My Girl* (1937). The story is of a poor London cockney who inherits a nobleman's title and fortune.

Irving Berlin was America's most popular composer since 1911, writing the songs to numerous stage reviews and films. The 1940s brought his first book musical to Broadway: *Louisiana Purchase* (1940).

Richard Rodgers and Oscar Hammerstein II paired up to write a stunning new musical. This duo set out to prove that a 'lyrics first' approach would make it easier to integrate the songs and the book of a show. This was something new – a fully-rounded musical play, with every element dedicated to moving the story forward. The show was named *Away We Go* and although it had potential, something was missing. At the suggestion of an ensemble member, a minor dance melody was re-set as a choral piece. When DeMille staged it with the chorus coming down to the footlights in a V formation singing 'O-K-L-A-H-O-M-A' – Oklahoma, a success was born.

Oklahoma! opened at New York's St. James Theatre on the night of March 31st, 1943. *Oklahoma!* is generally considered to be the first musical in the Golden Age of Broadway and therefore proved to be the pivotal point in the writing of book musicals.

Composers and lyricists now had to become dramatists. They needed to develop the characters and plot to create a story with colour and action. Dance routines were choreographed to help tell the show's story and the major characters had to be believable individuals. Not long after *Oklahoma!*, other songwriters turned their hand to this new way of approaching the musical – writing musical comedies with some serious undertones, adding choreographed movement and integrating every element into the storytelling process. However, achieving this wasn't as easy as it appeared and it was a long time before anyone else had the success of Rodgers and Hammerstein.

By the end of the 1940s integrated musical plays, both serious and comic, dominated the Broadway stage. The greatest composers in American popular music, Kurt Weill, Irving Berlin, Jule Styne and many more were all writing in this new Broadway style. Rodgers and Hammerstein, however, still had a great deal more to give. *South Pacific* (1949) confirmed their command of the genre. It won the Tony for Best Musical and became the second musical to receive the Pulitzer Prize for Drama.

In the 1950s they topped the billings with *The King and I* (1951), *Me and Juliet* (1953), *Pipe Dream* (1955), *Flower Drum Song* (1958) and finally *The Sound of Music* (1959).

Many other book musicals were produced in the 1950s, including Frank Loesser, Abe Burrows and Jo Swerling's very popular *Guys and Dolls* (1950) and Alan Jay Lerner and Frederick Loewe's *Paint Your Wagon* (1951), quickly followed by *My Fair Lady* (1956), an adaptation of George Bernard Shaw's *Pygmalion* starring Rex Harrison as Professor Higgins.

Dance was now becoming a major part of the musical. In Leonard Bernstein's *West Side Story* (1957) we see dance as very much an integral part of the plot. The *Romeo and Juliet* story is transported to modern day New York City and the feuding Montague and Capulet families are opposing ethnic gangs, the Sharks and the Jets. The book was adapted by Arthur Laurents, and the lyrics by Stephen Sondheim.

Laurents and Sondheim teamed up again for *Gypsy* (1959), with Jule Styne providing the music for a backstage story about the most driven stage mother of all time, stripper Gypsy Rose Lee's mother Rose.

The first project for which Sondheim wrote both music and lyrics was *A Funny Thing Happened on the Way to the Forum* (1962), with a book based on the works of Plautus by Burt Shevelove and Larry Gelbart. Later Sondheim's musicals left the stereotypical romantic plots of earlier eras and explored the grittier, darker side of life.

Thornton Wilder's play *The Matchmaker* was set to music by composer-lyricist Jerry Herman with the libretto by Michael Stewart and renamed *Hello Dolly!* (1964). This tells the story of a shrewd widow who brings young lovers together and finds a husband for herself in the New York of the1890s.

The Golden Age of Broadway came to a close with a number of memorable book musicals: *Funny Girl* (1964); *Fiddler on the Roof* (1964); *Mame* (1966); and of course *Cabaret* (1966). It is no wonder that these shows remain among the most performed musicals. Their stories and characters speak to the heart of human experience – the search for love in a harsh world and the triumph of the human spirit.

It was around the late 1960s that the musical started to again, mutate, and rock music was used in several Broadway book musicals, the first being Galt MacDermot's *Hair* (1968), which featured not only rock music but also nudity. *Hair* certainly shocked the musical scene and put even greater demands on the performers.

Composer, Andrew Lloyd Webber, and librettist, Tim Rice, took the first full rock musical, *Jesus Christ Superstar*, to the Broadway stage in 1971. With all the dialogue set to music, this work qualifies as the first rock opera. It was also the first of Andrew Lloyd Webber and Tim Rice's many blockbuster musicals.

Hot on the heels of *Jesus Christ Superstar* came Stephen Schwartz's *Godspell* (1971). The rock musical became a growing presence, with such big hits as *Grease* (1972) and *The Wiz* (1975), based on the story of *The Wizard of Oz*, but the American rock musical fashion soon died. The Broadway musicals were becoming huge, lavish, expensive productions that needed to keep reinventing themselves if they were to cover the costs at the box office.

Most of the new American book musicals in the mid-1970s met with disaster. The Broadway theatres went through a period of revamping the old show stopper with the 1971 revival of *No, No Nanette*, initiating a new craze for nostalgic musical revivals. The book musical was losing its popularity in America when in 1976 composer Charles Strouse, lyricist Martin Charnin and librettist Thomas Meehan made *Annie* an all-time box office success which ran solidly for six years.

The late 1970s gave us such Broadway musicals as John Kander and Fred Ebb's *Chicago* (1975) which relied on old vaudeville techniques, and Stephen Sondheim's *Sweeney Todd* (1979), a story of a man's all-consuming quest for revenge. This musical has a good storyline but a very ambitious operatic score. At the same time in Britain, the successful duo of Andrew Lloyd Webber and Tim Rice created *Evita* (1978), a serious political stage biography of Argentina's Eva Peron. *Evita* again is definitely a book musical but many of the songs became pop singles and hit the charts. Both *Sweeney Todd* and *Evita* were expensive productions with stunning staging and sets.

Andrew Lloyd Webber then went on to produce *Cats* (1981), based on the poems of T.S. Eliot and *The Phantom of the Opera* (1986), from the novel by Gaston Leroux, *Le*

Fantôme de l'Opéra. Other important writers of the 1980s and '90s include the French team of Claude-Michel Schönberg and Alain Boublil, responsible for *Les Misérables* and, in collaboration with Richard Maltby Jr., *Miss Saigon*, which takes its storyline from the opera *Madame Butterfly*.

We have also seen the Walt Disney Company turn some of their cartoon stories into spectacular musicals, such as *Beauty and the Beast* and *The Lion King*, and also create original stage productions like *Aida*, with music by Elton John. Disney continues to create new book musicals for Broadway and the West End theatres, most recently with its adaptation of its earlier film, *Mary Poppins*.

The latter part of the 20th Century saw many writers create smaller scale musicals, such as *Little Shop of Horrors* – based on the 1960 black comedy of the same name, *Bat Boy – the Musical* – based on Peter Bagge's cartoon story, *Adventures of Bat Boy*, in the Weekly World News, and *Blood Brothers*, with book, lyrics and music by Willy Russell. The growing scale and cost of some of the West End productions led to some concern that musicals had lost touch with the tastes of the general public, and that their costs were escalating beyond the budget of many theatregoers.

One of the most popular late 20th Century musicals is *Rent* by Jonathan Larson. It is based on the opera *La Bohème*, but the music is heavily rock-influenced, so that this is yet another book musical which falls between two genres.

The above named musicals are all based on books, stories or plays and can, therefore, be described as book musicals, but it is the nature and style of the individual songs that really classify them.

The 21st Century has seen the birth of two exciting new book musicals – *Wicked*, loosely based on characters from the story of *The Wizard of Oz* and *The Lord of the Rings*, based on Tolkien's classic. The former has already created a major impact and the success of the latter is yet to be measured. The interest that they have brought, however, has been profound. Others are yet to be created. The book musical is a category that may well overlap with other genres but, as long as plots and storylines provide inspiration, it is one that has a certain future.

DISCUSSION POINTS

• *What do you feel is the essence of a true book musical?*

• *What is thought to have been the first true book musical? What do you know about it?*

• *When was the Golden Age of the Broadway musical and why was it so called?*

• *Many of the most popular musicals have been book musicals. Can you name three, and give examples of any key songs within them?*

• *Which musical in the 1970s revived audience's waning interest in the book musical? Why do you think this happened?*

• *Which book musicals bridge two genres, for example 'crossing over' with operetta or rock/pop?*

REFERENCES

Everett, William A. & Laird, Paul R. (eds) – *The Cambridge Companion to the Musical* Cambridge University Press, 2002

Scholes, Percy A. & Ward, John Owen (ed) – *The Oxford Companion to Music* Oxford University Press, 1970

http://en.wikipedia.org

Chapter Six

Concept Musicals

DEFINITION

A concept musical is an idea or outline for a musical, which could be viewed as a work in progress, and can be in a semi-finished or finished form. It normally tells a story and appears first in a medium other than a fully-staged theatre or film musical.

A concept musical can be viewed as a try-out and can be recorded for an album or performed as a stage concert. The object could be to attract financial backing for further development.

An alternative view is that a concept musical is a musical which is built around a single concept or theme. Characters can perform songs which inform the audience about themselves and their nature. These songs support the theme rather than enhance the narrative and can describe elements which are not directly related to the central storyline. The characters can therefore comment on the subject and illustrate a variety of its aspects.

HISTORY

A concept musical album establishes and maintains a theme or story. The first concept album to be officially labelled as a rock opera was The Who's *Tommy* (June 1969, Track Records, UK Chart No.2) written mainly by Pete Townshend. He had already dabbled in this field with a track called 'A Quick One While He's Away' from The Who's second album *A Quick One* (Dec 1966, Reaction Records, UK Chart No.4). This was a nine minute suite of short songs telling a story in a rock opera form. However, *Tommy* was a double vinyl album, which told a story, although this was a little vague and incomplete. The lead single was 'Pinball Wizard' (Mar 1969, Track Records, UK Chart No.4). *Tommy* was performed either in part or in complete form at The Who's rock concerts.

Also in 1969, a 7-inch vinyl single of 'Superstar' from *Jesus Christ*, sung by Murray Head, was issued in a plain white cardboard sleeve with just the word 'Superstar' on the front. In spite of considerable airplay, the single failed to chart. In October 1970, a double vinyl concept album of *Jesus Christ Superstar* (MCA Records) was issued. It was billed as a rock opera with music by Andrew Lloyd Webber and lyrics by Tim Rice. The album reached No.1 in the US Chart (Dec 1970) and went on to sell 10 million copies worldwide, although it was not as successful in the UK. The Murray Head single reached US chart No.17 (June 1971) and was reissued in the UK as a 4 track maxi single (Jan 1972, UK Chart No.47), which also included 'I Don't Know How to Love Him' by Yvonne Elliman. By then, the song had already been covered and achieved hit status in the US for Helen Reddy and in the UK and France for Petula Clark ('La Chanson de Marie-Madeline', Disques Vogue). In February 1972, the concept album finally became successful in the UK (Chart No.6). After a series of live concert versions, the money raised from the album sales was used to fund the first stage production of a rock opera on Broadway in October 1971.

Stephen Sondheim's *Company* arrived on Broadway in April 1970, produced and directed by Harold Prince with choreography by Michael Bennett. *Company* has no real plot and creates a situation instead. It is based on a theme about marriage versus the single life.

In April 1971, the same team developed *Follies*, based on a theme of embittered marriages and bittersweet memories uncovered at a reunion of performers from a follies-style revue show. Harold Prince, in fact, resented these shows being labelled concept musicals, referring to them as 'unified' and 'integrated' shows.

On a religious theme, emerging in 1971, was the double vinyl box set concept album *Mass*. This is a musical theatre play for singers, players and dancers written by highly respected composer/conductor Leonard Bernstein, with lyrics by *Godspell* composer Stephen Schwartz. It was commissioned by the former First Lady, Jacqueline Kennedy, for the opening of the Kennedy Center for Performing Arts in Washington DC on September 8th 1971. It is based on the Tridentine Mass of the Roman Catholic Church and also featured a rock band performing rock and blues music.

Perhaps the most famous concept musical without a real plot is Michael Bennett's *A Chorus Line*, which opened on Broadway on July 25th 1975. Michael Bennett persuaded 24 dancers to talk into a tape recorder and give details of their backgrounds and audition experiences. He then gave the tapes to former dancer Nicholas Dante and playwright James Kirkwood to create a scenario based around the concept of a Broadway chorus audition. The fictional director of the show encourages the dancers to share their memories and innermost confidences. At the same time, composer Marvin Hamlisch and lyricist Edward Kleban developed songs which enhanced the characters' thoughts and feelings.

Vivian Ellis (1904–96), a well-known composer of musical theatre and songs became President of The Performing Rights Society in 1983. To celebrate his 80th birthday and to encourage the development of the musical, The Society, in conjunction with the Vivian Ellis Foundation, launched the Vivian Ellis Prize (1985–2000). The aim of the Foundation was 'to discover, nurture and promote writers in musical theatre working in Britain'. Applicants for the £3000 cash prize had to submit two or three songs, a sample of the dialogue and an outline of the story. These concept musicals were mainly in unfinished form. The finalists were judged at an annual showcase by a panel of professional musical theatre experts.

EXAMPLES

A Chorus Line: concept and direction by Michael Bennett; music by Marvin Hamlisch; lyrics by Edward Kleban; book by Nicholas Dante and James Kirkwood; original Broadway cast recording CBS/Sony Records.

The show was originally staged Off-Broadway at Joseph Papp's Public Theater. After 101 performances, it quickly moved to Broadway and the Schubert Theater, where it became 'a singular sensation'. It ran from July 25th 1975 to April 28th 1990 for 6137 performances and became the longest-running musical on Broadway. It won nine Tony Awards and the 1976 Pulitzer Prize for Drama – a rare feat for a musical. The London production opened on July 22nd 1976 at the Theatre Royal, Drury Lane, and ran for 903 performances. An American cast performed the show for six months before an all-British cast took over. The 1985 film directed by Richard Attenborough was less successful. It had two new songs replacing others, one of which, 'Surprise Surprise', was nominated for an Oscar. In October 2006, a major revival was staged on Broadway at the Gerald Schoenfeld Theater.

Captain Beaky and his Band: music by Jim Parker; lyrics by Jeremy Lloyd; Polydor Records.

A book of poems written by Jeremy Lloyd with illustrations by Keith Michell became an album with star performers in 1977. After time, the Captain Beaky track started to receive regular airplay on radio. It became a hit single with 'Wilfred the Weasel' in January 1980 (UK Chart No.5) and the album quickly moved up the album chart (No.28) in February, where it remained for three months. The success of the album slightly diminished the chances of the second single about a snake – 'The Trial of Hissing Sid' (UK Chart No.53) – although 'Hissing Sid is innocent' became a popular slogan and campaign. A second album with different star performers was released in 1980. The albums were turned into television concerts, a London West End musical and *Captain Beaky and his Musical Christmas* became a pantomime at the Apollo Theatre in December 1981.

Chess: music by Benny Anderson and Bjorn Ulvaeus; lyrics by Tim Rice; RCA Records.

The double vinyl concept album (Nov 1984, UK Chart No.10) took nine months to record at a cost of £500,000 and was launched by a series of platform concerts in London, Paris, Amsterdam, Hamburg and Stockholm all within the space of six days. It produced the hit singles 'One Night in Bangkok' by Murray Head (Nov 1984, UK Chart No.12; May 1985, US Chart No.3) which sold over 4 million copies worldwide, and 'I Know Him So Well' by Elaine Paige and Barbara Dickson (Jan 1985, UK Chart No.1) which became the second biggest selling single of 1985. The original story on the concept album was unclear and unfinished. Almost two years later, the London theatre production opened at the Prince Edward Theatre on May 14th 1986 with a revised plot and some new music. It was originally directed by Michael Bennett, who unfortunately had to withdraw as he became terminally ill, although this was unknown at the time. The direction was taken over by Trevor Nunn, who had to keep some of Michael Bennett's original concept and staging. The £4 million production ran until April 8th 1989 (1209 performances) and just recouped its costs. The Broadway production opened on April 28th 1988 at the Imperial Theater, directed by Trevor Nunn, who replaced most of the original ideas with a new heavier storyline with dialogue – the original had been sung through. Three new songs were added, including 'Someone Else's Story', and the running order of the remaining songs had been completely changed. The negative reaction of the US critics resulted in a huge financial failure and the show ran for just 68 performances. A Broadway cast album was released.

Company: concept and direction by Harold Prince; music and lyrics by Stephen Sondheim; book by George Furth; original Broadway cast recording CBS/Sony Records.

The show was built around the theme of marriage versus the single life. It opened on Broadway on April 26th 1970 at the Alvin Theater and ran for 705 performances. It won six Tony Awards and the songs have been recorded by many international artists. The American cast were brought to London and the show opened at Her Majesty's Theatre on January 18th 1972, where it ran for eight months and 344 performances. British replacements were brought in when the Americans left. In the 1990s, George Furth and Stephen Sondheim set about cutting and altering the dialogue to bring it up-to-date and they also rewrote the end of Act One. The 1995 Donmar Warehouse production starred Adrian Lester, who was the first black person to play Bobby. It ran from December 13th 1995 to March 2nd 1996 and then quickly transferred to the Albery Theatre from March 13th 1996 to June 29th 1996. There was a video broadcast of the production by BBC Television on March 1st 1997. The first act ended with the previously cut song 'Marry Me a Little' (see later in 'Examples') and this is now the accepted version of the show. A revival opened on Broadway on November 29th 2006 at the Ethel Barrymore Theater, directed by John Doyle, where the actors play the musical instruments as well. Mr Doyle had pioneered this concept in the UK and had a previously acclaimed production of Sweeney Todd in London and on Broadway using this style.

Dear Anyone: music by Geoff Stevens; lyrics by Don Black; book by Jack Rosenthal; DJM Records.

The story is about the life and times and letters sent to an agony aunt. When she becomes successful, her family life falls apart and she is forced to admit that she has the loneliest heart of all. The vinyl concept album was composed and released in 1978. It was performed by a variety of singers of the time including Maggie Moone, Murray Head and Steve Harley. The main theme song 'I'll Put You Together Again' was a hit single for the pop group Hot Chocolate in December 1978 (Rak Records, UK Chart No.13). The show received a London West End production at the Cambridge Theatre starring Jane Lapotaire, but it ran for just two months (Nov 8th 1983–Jan 7th 1984).

Evita: music by Andrew Lloyd Webber; lyrics by Tim Rice; MCA Records.

The 1976 double vinyl concept album (Jan 1977, UK Chart No.4) was based on the life of Eva Peron and used the London Philharmonic Orchestra. It produced the international hit single 'Don't Cry For Me Argentina' by Julie Covington (Dec 1976, UK Chart No.1), which was also a hit in Italy and France ('Le Chanson d'Evita', Disques Vogue) for Petula Clark. It also created the hit single, 'Another Suitcase in Another Hall', for Barbara Dickson (Feb 1977, UK Chart No.18). For the stage production, the storyline and some songs were changed, leaving out Che's attempt to sell insecticide to Argentina. The London production, directed by Harold Prince, starred David Essex, Elaine Paige and Joss Ackland and opened at the Prince Edward Theatre on June 21st 1978. It set a new West End theatre ticket price high of £6 and ran for 2900 performances, closing on February 8th 1986. The London cast album was also a success (Nov 1978, UK Chart No.24). The Broadway production at the Broadway Theater, starring Patti LuPone and Mandy Patinkin, opened in September 25th 1979 and ran for 1568 performances. After many years and cast changes, the film production finally secured financial backing and was released in 1996, starring Madonna, Antonio Banderas and Jonathan Pryce, and directed by Alan Parker. Andrew Lloyd Webber reluctantly had to considerably change the score to accommodate Madonna's vocal range. It did, however, contain a new song 'You Must Love Me' (Nov 1996, UK Chart No. 10) which won the Oscar for best song in 1997. A film cast album was released (Nov 1996, Warner Bros Records, UK Chart No.1) and 'Don't Cry For Me Argentina', coupled with a disco version, was a hit all over again for Madonna (Dec 1996, UK Chart No.3). She also had a subsequent hit with 'Another Suitcase in Another Hall' (Mar

1997, UK Chart No.7) which was the song originally sung by Peron's mistress. A major London revival at the Adelphi Theatre which opened on June 21st 2006 featured Elena Roger, the first Argentinian actress to play Eva Peron, and also included 'You Must Love Me'.

Jesus Christ Superstar: music by Andrew Lloyd Webber; lyrics by Tim Rice; MCA Records.

Please see 'History' for information on the 1970 concept album. The first stage production was at Broadway's Mark Hellinger Theater from October 1971 to June 1973. It ran for 711 performances and became Broadway's first fully-staged rock opera. A completely different and superior production opened at London's Palace Theatre on August 9th 1972 and ran for over eight years (3358 performances), becoming the longest running West End musical ever (London cast album) to be subsequently overtaken by another Andrew Lloyd Webber show, *Cats*. The musical was filmed in 1973 and directed by Norman Jewison (Soundtrack album, Sept 1973, UK Chart No.23). There have been two revivals on Broadway in 1977 and 2000. The 1996 London revival reopened the long dark Lyceum Theatre and produced another cast album. This production was also released on video and DVD.

Joseph and the Amazing Technicolor Dreamcoat: music by Andrew Lloyd Webber; lyrics by Tim Rice; MCA and Really Useful Records.

The show started out as a 15 minute lyric drama set to music for the choir of St. Paul's Junior School (Colet Court) in London. It had been commissioned by Alan Doggett, the then music master at the school. It was the first Lloyd Webber/Rice work to be performed in public on March 1st 1968. The piece was repeated in a concert at the Central Hall, Westminster some weeks later and was well-received by the press. The work was then expanded slightly and the first recorded version was 35 minutes long. The score was published and schools all over the UK began to perform it. American productions started to appear from 1969 onwards. These preceded longer versions in the UK, where the piece was extended to 90 minutes. In 1972, the first professional production directed by Frank Dunlop appeared at the Edinburgh Festival and then transferred to London's Young Vic Theatre in October (16 performances) before transferring again to The Roundhouse and Albery Theatres (243 performances). An album was recorded in 1973 (MCA Records) produced by Andrew Lloyd Webber and Tim Rice. It had no direct connection with any stage version, although the lead singers had all appeared in the Edinburgh production. The 1980 UK production became an enormous provincial hit and ranked as the longest ever post-war touring show, also making periodic appearances in London. The show finally arrived on Broadway at the Entermedia/Royale Theaters from November 1981 to September 1983 (824 performances) with a revival in November 1993 running until May 1994 (231 performances). Finally, 23 years after it was first performed, *Joseph* had its first hit single with 'Any Dream Will Do' by Jason Donovan (Jun 1991, Really Useful Records, UK Chart No.1) from the 1991 London Palladium revival (Stage cast album, Aug 1991, Really Useful Records, UK Chart No.1). Jason Donovan and other cast members also recorded a medley of songs to make the 'Joseph Mega Remix' (Dec 1991, UK Chart No.13) which became a popular party singalong. A DVD production starring Donny Osmond was then released. In April 2007, BBC Television launched *Any Dream Will Do*, a national search and TV competition for a new Joseph, to be chosen by the public to star in a new London production. The chairman of the judges was Andrew Lloyd Webber and the winner was Lee Mead.

Marry Me A Little: music and lyrics by Stephen Sondheim; concept by Craig Lucas and Norman Rene; RCA Records.

This is not a Stephen Sondheim musical. Craig Lucas was a member of the chorus of Sweeney Todd and during rehearsals Sondheim happened to mention the existence of some unperformed songs, some of which were out-takes from his previous works. When Lucas was commissioned to put together a musical revue, he asked permission to use some of the songs. Although Sondheim was very sceptical, he gave his permission and together they chose 17 songs. Working with director Norman Rene, Lucas conceived and developed the story of two single people who are alone in New York on a Saturday night. As the revue was performed on the set of another play, the characters were developed as young people moving into their first studio apartments, one above the other. The characters never meet. The show opened Off-Off-Broadway at The Production Company (Oct 29th 1980–Dec 28th 1980). It reopened Off-Broadway at the Actors' Playhouse on March 12th 1981 and ran for 96 performances. The RCA album was recorded on May 18th 1981. The London fringe production was at the King's Head Theatre (Jun 7th 1982–Jul 24th 1982). Since then, there have been numerous revivals in the US and UK. The title song 'Marry Me A Little', which was an out-take from *Company*, was reinstated into that show in 1995.

Mass: music by Leonard Bernstein; lyrics by Stephen Schwartz and Leonard Bernstein; additional lyrics by Paul Simon; Sony Records.

See 'History' for previous information. This theatre piece requires over 200 performers. It is a mixture of rock, jazz, electronic music and Gregorian chant, and the concept was somewhere between Broadway and opera. It is a very probing work about crisis in faith and the highly religious context made it very controversial. The European premiere was broadcast by BBC/PBS television in 1973. The US PBS television also broadcast the 10th anniversary production live from the Kennedy Center and a DVD Mass at the Vatican City is available of the June 2000 performance in front of an audience of 8000 people. Perhaps the most well-known song is 'The Simple Song' which was a major success for Petula Clark in France as 'Comme une prière' (Disques Vogue).

Mutiny!: music by David Essex; lyrics by Richard Crane and David Essex; book by Richard Crane; Mercury Records.

A major musical project from pop singer/actor David Essex was launched with the hit vinyl single 'Tahiti' (Aug 1983, UK Chart No.8). The double vinyl concept album with the Royal Philharmonic Orchestra (Oct 1983, UK Chart No.39) told the story of Captain Bligh, Fletcher Christian and the 1789 mutiny on the ship, HMS Bounty. The stars of the original album, David Essex and Frank Finlay, also starred in the London Piccadilly Theatre production directed by Michael Bogdanov, which arrived nearly two years later (Jul 22nd 1985–Sept 20th 1986). The production was promoted by a new song, 'Falling Angels Riding' (Feb 1985, UK Chart No.29). The London cast album (Telstar Records) was recorded in August 1985. The show is known for the set, designed by William Dudley, of the amazing stage recreation of HMS Bounty from a flat surface and for receiving a standing ovation at nearly every performance. The advertised transfer to Broadway did not happen.

Tell Me On a Sunday: music by Andrew Lloyd Webber; lyrics by Don Black; Polydor Records.

The first version was composed in New York with the concept that it would be a one-woman show about an ordinary English girl's love affairs and adventures in America. It was written for Marti Webb and the premiere was at the Sydmonton Festival in the summer of 1979. It was recorded and performed once in concert in January 1980. Also that month and rather unusually, the album was launched as a BBC TV concert. The huge success and popularity of the TV concert resulted in an almost immediate repeat showing, due to public demand. The concept album (Feb 1980, UK Chart No.2) produced the hit singles 'Take That Look Off Your Face' (Feb 1980, UK Chart No.3) and 'Tell Me On a Sunday' (Apr 1980, UK Chart No.67). In the autumn of 1981, the show was revised and expanded and a notable new song, 'The Last Man in My Life', was added. The song cycle emerged as a stage production as the 'song' part of 'Song and Dance', a theatre concert at the London Palace Theatre (Apr 7th 1982–Mar 31st 1984, 781 performances). The 'dance' part was to Andrew Lloyd Webber's 1978 Variations on Paganini's Caprice in A minor with a ballet company led by Wayne Sleep. Another new song, 'When You Want to Fall in Love' performed by Marti Webb and Wayne Sleep, was sung at the end to bring the two parts together. The first night was recorded and released as a live double album. When the show transferred to the Broadway Royale Theater (Sept 18th 1985–Nov 8th 1986, 474 performances) the lyrics had to be substantially altered to accommodate a new character for Bernadette Peters. New lyrics were also put to the music of 'When You Want to Fall in Love' and this became the notable 'Unexpected Song'. The Broadway album was issued under the title 'Song and Dance – The Songs'. The show was revised, updated and extended again with five new songs and additional material by Jackie Clune for the most recent London production. It was designed as a showcase for Denise Van Outen (Gielgud Theatre, Apr 15th 2003–Feb 14th 2004) and was restaged under the original title of *Tell Me on a Sunday*.

Tommy: music and lyrics by Pete Townshend; Track Records.

See 'History' for previous information on the 1969 rock opera album. After the opera had been performed as a Who rock concert, a new project emerged in late 1972 with the London Symphony and English Chamber Orchestras and a symphonic version of Tommy was recorded with leading pop and rock stars of the day. From this came the hit single 'I'm Free' for Roger Daltrey (Aug 1973, Ode Records, UK Chart No.13). The new album was promoted with stage shows in 1973. Pete Townshend had to rework the storyline and change some key elements for the 1975 film directed by Ken Russell (Apr 1975, Polydor Records, UK Chart No.21). 'Pinball Wizard' became a hit again, but this time for Elton

John (Mar 1976, DJM Records, UK Chart No.7). A fully-staged theatre production was mounted at Broadway's St. James Theater (Apr 22nd 1993–June 18th 1995, 899 performances) 24 years after the original album. Again, the lyrics required several rewrites, the numbers were reorganised and a new song was added. The key plot elements changed for the film were reversed to the original storyline. The show won five Tony Awards including best original score. The London production arrived at the Shaftesbury Theatre March 5th 1996 and ran until February 8th 1997.

YET TO BE STAGED

Here are some examples of concept musicals that have not progressed any further beyond the original concept album. These albums feature singers who are unlikely to portray the roles on stage. They are used merely to promote and sell the records and individual songs.

Goya... A Life in Song: music and lyrics by Maury Yeston; CBS/Sony Records.

Placido Domingo was very keen to create a work about the life of Spanish painter Francisco de Goya. He collaborated with Maury Yeston, Tony Award winning composer of *Nine* and *Titanic*. It was written in 1987 and the concept recording was released in 1989 featuring, among others, Placido Domingo, Gloria Estefan and Dionne Warwick. The love theme from Goya; 'Till I Loved You'; became an international hit duet for Barbara Streisand and Don Johnson (Nov 1988, CBS Records, UK Chart No.16). The stage production was frequently mentioned on televised industry award shows, but to date has not received a major staging.

Little Tramp: music and lyrics by David Pomeranz; WEA Records.

The story is based on the life of Charlie Chaplin and also highlights the time when he was prevented from re-entering the US due to alleged political and moral charges. The CD was released in 1992 with a cast of famous names including

Mel Brooks, Petula Clark, Tim Curry and Richard Harris. It is understood that work is still in progress on this project.

Rage of the Heart: music and lyrics by Enrico Garzilli; First Night Records.

The story is based on the lives of Abelard and Heloise. The double album, released in 1989, featured Michael Ball and Janet Mooney in the title roles. This is now a very rare and valuable vinyl album.

DISCUSSION POINTS

• *What is a concept musical?*

• *What do you know about the significance of songs within a concept musical?*

• *What do you know about the place of characters within a concept musical as opposed to characters in any other genre of musical?*

• *Which is the most famous concept musical without a real plot?*

• *Which concept musical was built around a book of poems? What do you know about it?*

• *Name any concept musicals composed by Andrew Lloyd Webber and discuss their history and journey.*

REFERENCES

Kennedy, Michael, Muir, John & Bunnett, Rexton S. – *Collins Guide to Musicals* HarperCollins, 2001

Roberts, David – *Guinness World Records: British Hit Singles & Albums* Guinness World Records Limited, 2007

The Vivian Ellis Foundation

www.ibdb.com

www.musicals101.com

www.musicals.net

www.thisistheatre.com

http://en.wikipedia.org

Chapter Seven

Pop and Rock Musicals

DEFINITION: POP MUSICAL

At the end of the 20th Century more and more musical 'styles' have been re-worked into the form of the 'Musical'. There are many reasons for this, the main one being commercial with the need for good box office returns. As a result of this cross-fertilisation, the pop/rock genre generally defies definition because neither part of the hybrid musical equation finds it easy to be labelled. Often the works straddle other forms, resulting in confusion when trying to place musicals within a specific genre. However, for the purposes of examination work rather than academic classification the 'pop' (popular of the day) element may be defined as any musical that reflects the past glories of popular music. This aspect of reflection has been explored throughout the entire development of musical theatre. A good example would be the musical *Anything Goes* (1934) where each song, penned by Porter, in each different version of the same show throughout its performance history has included different songs from that of the previous version, eg 1962, 1987 and 2004 productions.

Later there were musicals reflecting the popular music of the past such as *Tintypes* (1979), a nostalgic musical revue looking back to the first decade of the 20th Century (pre 1917) that included such popular songs as 'You're a Grand Old Flag,' 'Meet Me in St Louis', 'Yankee Doodle Boy' and 'Radio Hour' (1979) which featured the music of the early 1940s Hit Parade.

All pop musicals have an essential retrospective ingredient, looking back with affection, evoking atmospheres and memories for present-day audiences. It is therefore not surprising that the popular concept of recycling has become an inevitable part of the history and development of the musical as we know it in the 21st Century.

DEFINITION: ROCK MUSICAL

The rock musical has its birth in the 1960s and it is generally accepted that *Hair* (1968) was the first such musical to incorporate all the elements of a rock score. However, *Bye, Bye Birdie* (1960), based around the hysteria created by Elvis Presley entering the Armed Forces, may also be considered by some as the first rock musical for much the same reasons, eg rock'n'roll elements within the score. Whether early or late '60s, it is from this decade that the journey exploring this form must begin.

Two distinctive features of nearly all rock musicals were, firstly, the distinct lack of a viable narrative (the music alone not giving sufficient gravitas to make the rock musical an enduring feature within the overall genre of the musical) and, secondly, the removal of the fourth wall as in a traditional concert forum. The removal of the fourth wall was clearly an ingredient to be explored within this genre of musical, mainly because the sung material directly related to the audience and there was a believable connection with the actor/singer and their audience. This is an essential ingredient when considering the preparation of song material for performance, especially such aspects as spontaneity and textual relevance to the singer of the song. However, there are some musicals within the genre that do break new ground and allow us to use the tag, 'rock musical', with confidence and academic security.

As our studies take us along the path of discovery we will begin to realise that the actual pop/rock classification takes us to a point where generic terms such as the 'tribute' and 'juke box' musicals become more common terminology. This happened within the last decade of the 20th Century and they are still current in the world of contemporary musical theatre.

Let the journey begin…

The first half of the musical equation, 'pop', had its greatest growth in the 1980s and '90s when audiences in their mid-40s went to the theatre to listen to familiar music of their youth rather than attempting to listen to 'new' original musical theatre material. Composers like Sondheim appear to have suffered from this sociological approach to the musical, with several of his shows only lasting a few performances before being revived and finally announced as masterpieces of the 20th Century!

Grease (1972), remains one of the most popular musicals of the 20th Century, running for 3,388 performances. It is considered as a pop musical because of its musical score and reliance on pastiche and the easily recognisable rock'n'roll music sound and style.

The innovative and essentially 'British' musical, *The Rocky Horror Show* (1973), used the music popular of the day and has made a considerable contribution to the culture of musicals. In the late 1970s and early '80s there were three shows which were directly based on 'popular' music. They are as follows: *Ain't Misbahavin* (1978), a black cast show based on the music of Fats Waller, *Eubie* (1979), based around the music of Eubie Blake, and *Sophisticated Ladies* (1981), where a Duke Ellington night club act is brought to life on a Broadway stage.

In 1978 Bob Fosse created a musical which was to do for popular dance forms what other musicals did for popular song. *Dancin'* was an evocation of the past glories of Fosse's dance styles and as a result had a specific cachet for the audiences of the day. It was an obvious commercial ploy but despite this was a success, running for over 1,500 performances.

The Sugar Babies (1979) gave a revue-type musical look at the past with such songs as 'I Feel a Song Coming On' and 'I Can't Give you Anything but Love'.

First seen as a film in the late 1930s, *42nd Street* could also be considered as a pop musical as it refers to many of the old songs already made famous and popular in the '30s such as the classic 'Lullaby of Broadway' and 'We're in the Money'.

Another musical born in the UK that inhabits the world of pop and rock musicals in style, if not in songs, is the wonderful and most moving *Blood Brothers* (1982), still seen in the West End today.

Leader of the Pack came to the stage in 1985. A musical based upon the very important composer/lyricist Ellie Greenwich; it featured at least 20 of her previous hits from the 1960s.

Beehive (1986), a musical based upon the hairstyle of the 1950s and '60s, honoured the music of the period and featured the work of such vocal artists as Aretha Franklin and Petula Clark. Other musicals that continued in this theme were as follows: *Uptown* (1986), a dance revue similar to *Dancin'* but about the dance of a previous age, not one choreographer, and a musical entitled *Honky Tonk Nights* (1986) that reflected the old black vaudeville shows of the past and so captured the once 'popular' music of a bygone age.

In 1987 *Stardust* might have encouraged the general audience to consider this to be the first tribute musical, but it was not to be. Again, it was a compilation of songs by the lyricist Mitchell Parrish putting together a revue that used pop material and such songs as 'Stardust' and 'Sophisticated Lady'. A result of material being familiar, the musical was clearly commercially viable and was well-received by its audiences, running for about a year on Broadway.

On a matter of historical note it is interesting to note that these pop musicals often appear at a time when original material is lacking. The year 1989 on Broadway is an example where no musical was awarded any 'gongs' or awards. However, in the same year, two commercial ventures were opened. The first was entitled *Black and Blue*, which consisted of a thin storyline and jazz and blues numbers from the past, and the second, Jerome Robbins' *Broadway*, a revisit of a similar tried format to that of *Dancin'*, already mentioned above, but this time looking at work by Jerome Robbins. It is not surprising that at this moment in the history of the musical it was necessary for the Tony awards to add another category to their illustrious collection and to award 'best revival' – no more need be said!

Forever Plaid (1990) is a musical that continued to evoke the atmosphere of the 1960s and acknowledged the crossover from the boy bands of the '50s (and even '40s) to the era of the Beatles. This musical contains the most exquisite arrangements of such popular songs as 'Catch a Falling Star', 'Magic Moments' and 'Three Coins in a Fountain'.

Later in the same year a musical that is still with us was performed for the first time – *Buddy: The Buddy Holly Story* (1990). This was a musical recreation of the life and music of Buddy Holly. Songs included in the show are, to name a few; 'That'll be the Day', 'Johnny B. Goode' and a further selection from the other two artists who were unfortunately killed in the same crash, Big Bopper and Ritchie Valens – 'Chantilly Lace' and 'La Bamba'.

One failure was the musical entitled *Back to Bacharach and David* (1993) by Burt Bacharach and Hal David, which received only 69 performances and evoked their most prolific period of song writing with such popular songs as 'Do You Know the Way to San Jose', 'Close to You' and 'I'll Never Fall in Love Again'. Another musical written by the same duo, *Promises, Promises*, although not really appropriate for this category, actually did contribute to the development of the musical by making it an expectation that sounds heard in the theatre were identical to those on a commercial recording. Perhaps this was the reason that writers such as Andrew Lloyd Webber, Paul Simon and The Who, who all cut concept albums as a first venture, before producing *Jesus Christ Superstar*, *The Capeman* and *Tommy* on either the West End or Broadway. It is certainly well-documented that the concept album of *Notre Dame*, performed in the West End in 2000, was a concept album first and actually gained an entry in the *Guinness Book of Records* for being the most successful show in its first year of performance.

Another popular musical by Leiber and Stoller, both 'giants' in their day within the world of music, is still currently being performed and in receipt of good audiences. It is the wonderful *Smokey Joe's Café* (1995), which at first strike achieved a record of well over 2,000 performances. Songs such as 'Hound Dog', 'Fools Fall in Love' and 'Spanish Harlem' are essential ingredients in this pop retrospective musical celebrating the music of the late 1950s and '60s.

As in *Tintypes* (1979), which evoked the music of the early 20th Century with considerable affection and all that it meant to the world of the Americas, in the 1990s the memories of those who took part in World War II were at their highest. This period rapidly became a fascination for the next generation, including the popular music of the day. The musical *Swingtime Canteen* (1995) was such an evocation of the past and this time had at its centre a girl's vocal group, similar to *Forever Plaid* five years previously. Recollections of the girl band in *Some Like It Hot* come rapidly to mind as we consider the vocal music of the period with such examples as the popular 'Boogie Woogie Bugle Boy'.

Then, in the latter part of the 1990s, there were a series of musical revues featuring the music of Johnny Burke in *Swinging on a Star* (1995) and the music of Johnny Mercer in *Dream* (1997). To complete the '90s there was a musical that evoked the mood of the dance of the previous decades. In the musical revue, *Swing* (1999), the era of the 1930s and '40s were once again revisited – presumably before the audiences could no longer remember these as part of their youth.

Mamma Mia (1999) is a great example of this new hybrid of the pop musical, incorporating 27 ABBA songs. Although the musical contains the songs of ABBA the storyline is distinct and follows the world of Donna and her daughter Sophie. It links the songs together in a most imaginative manner and it is in this musical that we can see ways of working with material to be discussed later. For example, in the song 'The Winner Takes It All', the character of the mother places the song within a different context to the original conception and now relates it to bringing up a child – an imaginative way of re-working the material. Above all, this musical is well-crafted and has a strong storyline and an excellent set of musical material to advance the narrative. Unfortunately, the same cannot be said for most of the list mentioned below.

Additional pop musicals that contribute to the genre and evoke the spirit or refer to the musical 'numbers' of the past are as follows:

A Slice of Saturday Night, Heather Brothers, 1992

Boogie Nights, Motown Music '70s, 1997

Saturday Night Fever, Bee Gees, 1999

Movin' Out, Billy Joel, 2002

Our House, Madness, 2002

We Will Rock You, Queen, 2002

Dream a Little Dream, The Mamas and Papas, 2003

Stand by Your Man, Tammy Wynette, 2003

Tonight's the Night, Rod Stewart, 2003

Promises and Lies, UB40, 2004

The Rat Pack, Various music associated with Sinatra/Martin/Davis, 2005

Good Vibrations, Beach Boys, 2005

All Shook Up, Elvis Presley, 2005

Lennon, John Lennon, 2005

Jersey Boys, Franki Valli/Four Seasons, 2005

Almost Heaven, John Denver, 2005

Ring of Fire, Bob Dylan, 2006

The Genius of Ray Charles, Ray Charles, 2006

The Melody Lingers On, Irving Berlin, 2006

Don't Make Me Over, Dionne Warwick, 2006

Dancing In the Streets, Motown Music, 2006

Sinatra, Frank Sinatra, 2006

Daddy Cool, Boney M, 2006

Desperately Seeking Susan, Blondie & Deborah Harry, 2007

With many of the above-mentioned musicals, the original sung material is often never intended to be in a piece of musical theatre and so the songs are shoe-horned into the fabric of the storyline as best as possible. The book written to identify the narrative is often false in its objective and so the link between song and narrative is minimal. Although there are always notable exceptions, there is often little doubt that the songs are the sole reason for the musical being created and performed at all.

THE FUTURE...

The reflection of the past has always been an important aspect of the musical genre and recently film has become the genre to revisit. The film by Frank Capra, *Meet John Doe*, is set as a musical by the brilliant Richard Maltby together with a book by Andrew Gerle. It evokes the music of the '60s including 'Chapel of Love' and 'The Times They are A-Changin''. It is noted that Maltby dislikes the term 'jukebox musical' because it 'suggests a random collection of tunes – a concert.' It is yet to be seen in the UK and, if and when it is, we will then be able to judge the validity of his thoughts. However, the combination of Maltby and Gerle promises many riches and much excitement if we actually get to see it!

THE ROCK MUSICAL: 'THIS IS THE DAWNING OF THE AGE OF AQUARIUS...'

The decade of the 1960s – what an exciting moment in our history! Consider yet again, the concept of '*Anything Goes*' and we have the '60s! Society is released from its chains and at the closing of the decade the laws prohibiting nudity on stage were repealed as well as important laws regarding the presentation and re-presentation of Christ. It is therefore not surprising that such musicals as *Jesus Christ Superstar* and *Godspell* were to reach the stage at the dawn of the '70s. This surely was the '…age of Aquarius!'

Having suggested previously that the first rock musical might be considered as *Bye, Bye Birdie* it is quite clear that the most brilliant and important musical of this genre was *Hair* (1967). Even the subtitle does not allow the form to go unannounced – 'An American Tribal Love-Rock Musical.' Despite a very long inception and years of draft working versions, it eventually saw the light of day and became iconic within the field of musical theatre. *Hair* evoked ideas of free expression reflecting the Hippie fashion and dance explosion, for example, as in BBC's Top of the Pops, featuring dance groups such as Pan's People. Within this musical we were to witness the beginnings of cross fertilisation between the small screen and the stage. Its weakness was to be the fact that it did not have a worthy narrative. Both *Hair* and *Grease*, the latter a musical soon to change the face of the musical for each new generation of audience, celebrate the world of drugs, racial tolerance and all things appertaining to the decade of the 1960s. We, as an audience, have to decide whether this is a good or bad thing in the light of our own cultural development and to take a new look at such issues within contemporary society.

Hair has a clear preoccupation with the music of the '60s and the heavy amplified rock sounds and bass line was responsible for promoting at least four of its songs to the current hit parade as was then – these were 'Hair', 'Good Morning Sunshine', 'Let the Sunshine In' and 'Aquarius'. Unfortunately, following on from *Hair*, any show using rock music would be labelled a rock musical, eg *I'm Getting My Act Together and Taking It on the Road* and as a result the form becomes slightly confused by its overuse.

In addition to the use of a specific style of music, there was one more factor that linked these musicals together in a similar genre; the discussion and raising of 'issues' such as the treatment of war and the problems of growing up in today's society. However, there are notable exceptions and references to them will be made later in this section.

Musicals that deserve classification and further research, for one reason or another, are as follows:

Bye, Bye Birdie, Strouse, 1960

Hair, Rado/Ragni/MacDermott, 1967

Salvation, Link/Courtney, 1969

Oh! Calcutta!, Various composers inc. Shikele/Dennis/Walden, various writers inc. Beckett/Lennon/Shepard, 1969

Georgy, George Fischoff, 1970

Two Gentlemen of Verona, MacDermott, 1971

Your Own Thing, MacDermott, 1972

Dude, MacDermott, 1972/3

Via Galactica, MacDermott, 1973

Some of the above marked musicals ran for very few performances but are still recognised and recorded within the category of rock musical:

Jesus Christ Superstar, Webber/Rice, 1971

Godspell, Stephen Schwartz, 1971

Grease, Jacobs/Caset, 1972

Sgt Pepper's Lonely Hearts Club Band on the Road, The Beatles, 1974

The Wiz, Brown/Smalls, 1975

Beatlemania, The Beatles, 1977

I'm Getting My Act Together and Taking It on the Road, Cryer/Ford, 1978

Dreamgirls, Motown Music Collaborations, 1981

Chess, Andersson/Ulvaeus/Rice, 1988

Buddy: The Buddy Holly Story, Buddy Holly, 1989

Tommy, The Who, 1993

Faust, Randy Newman, 1996

Rent, Larsen, 1996

The Capeman, Paul Simon/Derek Walcott, 1998

Hedwig and the Angry Inch, Mitchell/Trask, 1998

Notre Dame de Paris, Richard Cocciante, 2000 (although its artistic team always described it as 'The Musical Spectacular' within the marketing material)

Both *Jesus Christ Superstar* and *Godspell* deal with the same aspect of Jesus' last days on earth (both having very different ways of exploring the narrative) and are influenced by different aspects of modern day rock-style music. Their success reflected the social current at the time and so encouraged a sense of spiritual revival within society and aspects of 'good' to be appreciated within the world.

The musical *Jesus Christ Superstar* had one more thing to offer the world of the musical that had never really been explored fully before, the potential to disturb the rhythms within the score and to immediately disturb the heartbeat of the listener. This was powerfully dramatic and time signatures such as 7/8 and 5/4 were crucial in the sub-textual references within the music being performed. This is in some ways as innovative as the Sondheim 'concept' musical, *A Little Night Music*, written entirely in 3/4 time and so making all thoughts and ideas be bound by a rhythmic structure that in its turn creates tensions and musical interest to be appreciated by the audience.

Songs from *Godspell* remain ever popular such as the beautiful and evocative 'Day by Day'. The other important issue arising from the musical *Godspell* was the removal of the fourth wall. With this there was not only a hint of what was to come with regard to the rock musical but also a reflection of such practitioners as Bertolt Brecht (who also wrote plays of a didactic nature and so encouraged the removal of the fourth wall as an essential feature when connecting with an audience).

Perhaps the most well-known musical of the 20th Century is *Grease* (1972), which incorporates elements of both pop and rock from the era of the '50s. This musical reflects both the sexual and social revolution within America. There is a useful comparison to be made in the satirical content of both *Grease* and *Bye, Bye Birdie*. In *Bye, Bye Birdie* the character of Birdie is a clear caricature of Elvis Presley and tells of the problems associated with him entering the Armed Forces. In *Grease*, we see the glorification of the youth obsession with sex and drugs, especially when we witness the character of Sandy abandoning her previous prim and proper ways of living to achieve a sexual and social fulfilment. One wonders how prophetic this musical actually is and why is it so popular with the generation of today?

The Wiz (1975) was referred to by critics as a rock musical and supported an all-black cast framed around the storyline of a previous musical, *The Wizard of Oz*. Perhaps the most famous song from the show was the popular 'Ease on Down the Road'.

One musical that cannot go unmentioned is the fantastic re-working of Puccini's *La Bohème* in the musical *Rent*. John Larsen uses contemporary issues to explore the same points as in the opera but allows the heroine Mimi, whom we know is dying, to live on beyond the final curtain thus giving a sense of hope and anticipation to the needs of society. Not only is this musical a significant milestone in the genre of rock musicals but in terms of presentation, we have a replication of what had happened earlier in the musical *Promises, Promises*, where the sound engineer's work is of paramount importance to recreate a 'live' sound in the theatre that reflects the 'rock' idiom and so impacts upon the theatre audience. *Rent* requires the performers to make a clear connection with both speech and song in order to communicate the truth of the dramatic situation. This is perhaps the most well-formed and structured piece of work within the entire genre of 'rock' musicals and reflects the development of vocal treatments to be employed within the world of musical theatre.

DISCUSSION POINTS

• *How would you define the classification 'pop' musical?*

• *Why is Grease one of the most popular musicals of the 20th Century? What do you know about it?*

• *Which pop musical incorporated 27 ABBA songs? Why has it been so popular?*

• *What is a rock musical?*

• *Why was the 'Age of Aquarius' so important in the development of the rock musical? Can you give any examples from this period?*

• *Why is Rent a significant milestone in the evolvement of musical theatre?*

REFERENCES

Boardman, G., *American Musical Theatre* Oxford University Press, 1992

Everett, W.A. & Laird, P.R. (eds.), *The Cambridge Companion to the Musical* Cambridge University Press, 2002

Ganzl, K., *The Musical: A Concise History* Northeastern University Press, 1997

Jones, John B., *Our Musicals, Ourselves: A Social History of the American Musical Theater* Brandeis University Press, 2003

The Stage, Journal

Chapter Eight

Preparation for LAMDA Examinations

The following chapter suggests how to approach the LAMDA Musical Theatre for the Actor/Singer Examinations. It is by no means prescriptive and demonstrates only some of the ways of tackling examination requirements.

PREPARATION FOR LAMDA EXAMINATIONS

In terms of preparation the world is your oyster and quite literally – *Anything Goes*! To take a song with a current popularity and to trial the acting process as an actor/singer is one of the most suitable means of working towards the goal of these examinations.

However, for the sole purpose of the examination itself it is essential that the song chosen must also be referenced within another more structured performance context, ie the musical. The reason for this being that there has to be a recognised journey for the song. The transference of song from one genre into another is something to discuss in terms of both the creation and context of the musical. This will also allow the examiner and the candidate the opportunity to have common ground upon which to discuss the artistic value of the song being presented for the exam and the integration within an accepted musical form.

It is essential that any song from any genre of musical can be placed within two contexts (i) the original artiste and performance date and (ii) the musical to which it now belongs and any other relevant information.

Many of the categories we have discussed are constantly changing and we can find elements of many different genres within a single musical. As a student it is vital that you make a detailed study of the form, content and history of your chosen musical in order to ensure that your work and your chosen song is worthy of assessment. Simply knowing a category or singing a song is only the first five minutes of your journey.

Remember that whatever song you have chosen to present you MUST be able to answer these three questions: 'Who are you?' 'Where are you?' 'What is happening to you?' In other words, place your work firmly in a context and make certain that your performance skills are as technically assured as they would be in your understanding of any acting style. Make sure that all choices made within the performance of the song create an interesting character in all senses of the word.

PERFORMANCE PROCESS

With reference to all musicals, as the actor/singer we are required to look at the ingredients of the actual song and then bring our acting skills to the task of presenting it to an audience. As stated earlier, the song 'The Winner Takes It All' sung as a pop song by ABBA, has a completely different context to the way it is played within the actual show of *Mamma Mia*. Always remember to explore the full potential of the lyric first and then create an environment and place for the song to have a full and purposeful meaning.

Remember: Singing the song for its own sake is not enough in musical theatre.

THE BEGINNING OF THE JOURNEY OF DISCOVERY

Select the song from the musical of your choosing.

You might like to check the song over by listening to it but please remember the song heard is that singer's version, not yours.
You must not rely on the version you hear – you are now to be the creator of this song and a detailed acting process must be undertaken in order to create the spontaneity required to make your work shine through! (Having listened to the song – leave well alone!)

Write out the words of the song by hand – do not type or word process – there is little or no connection within this activity. You must make a direct connection with each word of the song as you place them on the page – it will help you remember them as well! Write out the lyric in continuous prose without punctuation and reference to the verse structure if either exists!

BRINGING THE TEXT TO 'LIFE'

Speak this monologue several times, aiming to create as many different 'attitudes' towards the lyrics on each version of the performance. Note down all the differences by recording yourself performing these.

Decide whether the monologue is about (i) your feelings (ii) telling your story or communicating a 'special' moment in your life (iii) expressing a lesson to be learnt by your experiences in life (teaching song) or (iv) engaging with the audience regarding something that moves you which you want to share at the precise moment of singing.

MAKING DECISIONS

Continue to investigate the lyric as a monologue and discover a reason for being able to speak the first phrase at the beginning of the song. What inspires you to speak the first line?

Ask yourself at the end of the song – are you thinking in the same way or has the substance and meaning of the lyric changed for whatever reason?

Ask questions in every silence – why the pause? What thought is being encouraged?

When you have made some decisions about the dramatic significance of the song, look at the way the lyricist has written out the words and obey the punctuation marks as written. Do you agree or have all your performance versions been different? No problem, but now you have to agree to 'go with the lyricist'. This process will surely make you recognise something different about this song and its sense of purpose that you had not recognised for whatever reason.

A NEW DIRECTION

Perform the lyric again as a dramatic monologue, obeying in every detail the punctuation and phrasing. Pay attention to every detail of the writing and any changes in direction of thought.

It is important to remember that the lyricist and composer have already completed this work for you so you must respect this work and contribute something to the creation of the song chosen for performance – otherwise what are you really doing?

Is it different now – how different?

Every time you must record your work or you will convince yourself that there has been no difference at all between any of the performances given. You must also write down your responses. This is an 'active' way of learning for the actor/singer. The journey of discovery can easily be forgotten if you fail to give it respect or to recognise change when it occurs or even why it occurs! This method of approaching the song will give you invaluable discussion material to have with your examiner when he/she observes and questions your performance decisions towards the end of the examination. Remember if you keep your mind continually active you will know why and what you are doing.

THE TECHNICAL ASPECTS OF THE SONG: WHAT IS REALLY GOING ON?

Having spoken the monologue and come to terms with the content, it is useful to have a good look at the score and go through it whilst listening to a performance or observing a pianist playing the accompaniment. Listen out for such things as follows:

- How many bars are there before I start to sing?

- What is happening in the accompaniment whilst I am singing?

- Is it in a major or minor key – why?

- Does it change key – what impact does this have to the song – where does the change of key take place?

- What am I thinking while the musical introduction is playing?

- What happens throughout the song when I am not singing?

- How many pauses are there?

- What am I to think in each pause?

- At the end of the song, do I sing until the end or does the piano finish off the song?

When you have considered some of the above details, and hopefully even more, you are ready to perform the song in a spoken delivery, accessing the entire content, form and structure of the song. All too often performers are totally unaware of 'when to come in' or 'how the music goes' at the end of the song! It is your job as an actor to know what supports your work and honour the entire process, not just the work of your own voice!

N.B. It would be helpful to make up your own list of questions in order that your performance work becomes individual to your own ways of working.

DEVELOP TECHNICAL ASPECTS WITHIN THE SONG

One exercise to help this process would be to recite the song and clap the rhythm of the opening and the intervening passages where you do not sing! Consider the detailed map of the song and identify what you are to do within each one of the so-called 'gaps in the music.' This will really allow you to interrogate the qualities within the song and give you a sense of the internal rhythm driving the song. All too often singing unaccompanied reveals the true understanding of the song and the true ability of the performer. Do not rely on the accompaniment to 'push' you through.

As a result of this work you will also be better prepared to make use of the first time you meet an accompanist or repetiteur to assist you in the learning of the musical phrases, eg the notes of the song – the simplest and by far the easiest bit of the process!

PUTTING IT TOGETHER – FURTHER EXERCISES

Having learnt the notes/melody of the song you have now reached the exciting point at which you can put the work into the performance space and so bring all your hard work to fruition. However, first you must make sure that you are in control of the song, not the song in control of you. An exercise to help you do this would be to speak the song with accurate attention to detail of rhythm and rests within the music by (i) walking in the rhythm of the song whilst speaking it and (ii) repeating the same exercise but this time walking or jogging in a completely different tempo whilst maintaining the 'flow' of the lyric as in the first exercise. Have fun! Again it would be useful to recognise and write down what you have learnt about this song when you have completed this work.

PHYSICALISATION OF THE SONG

Now to understand the physicality of your character or yourself whilst singing this song – you must discover what habitual gestures you are not aware of. Consider these exercises as helpful to access this aspect of the work:

• Are there any clues as to your physicality within the lyrics of the song?

• How does the setting you have created for your song give a reason for movement or stillness?

• Do the movements have reference to the period of the song, eg 1920s/'60s?

• How does your specific interpretation impact upon the movement of the singer?

BACK TO THE TEXT

Return to the text and underline the important words, ie subject and verb. This will help you understand the importance of certain words rather than be persuaded to reinforce the high note in the melodic phrase that is actually to be sung on the word 'and'. Too many times we are aware of the beautiful melody but the meaning of the song has been lost at its expense!

MAKING THE SONG YOUR OWN!
DEFINING YOUR PERFORMANCE AND INTENTIONS

Now the thoughts have been determined, you can mark your breathing points and the quality of creativity that is required to make sense of the words yet to be sung. This is necessary because the quality of breath supporting the thought is paramount in this work – there can be no errors here! The technical preparation will finally 'release' the work and so create a wonderful 'alive' and personal piece of work – thus encouraging you to create an original interpretation of a 'classic' song.

Good luck with your examination and enjoy the journey!